W̵ ⁜ïïne

In 1995 The Rt Revd Brother Michael Fisher SSF
celebrated fifty years as an Anglican Franciscan.
Throughout his ministry he has travelled extensively
in Britain and worldwide, preaching in universities,
schools and parishes. Within the Franciscan
movement he has held the position of Provincial
Minister and Minister General of the worldwide
Anglican Franciscan Order. From 1979 to 1985 he
was Bishop of St Germans in the Diocese of Truro,
Cornwall, and from 1985 to 1996 Assistant Bishop in
the Diocese of Ely. Known to a wide circle within
and outside the Anglican church as "Brother
Michael", his sermons and addresses have made a
lasting impression on all who hear them.

*"A beautifully real book. There is not a word in it,
whether addressed to 2000 young people in
Portsmouth Cathedral or to a gathering of
Archbishop Primates prior to a Lambeth Conference
or to Diocesan clergy wives in Ely on bereavement
or at the Annual Rose Festival in Wisbech, which
does not come out of Brother Michael's frontier experience."*

The Rt Revd PETER WALKER

Preach the Word. Be instant;
In season out of season.

Second Epistle to Timothy

A sentence uttered makes a world appear
Where all things happen as it says they do:
We doubt the speaker, not the tongue we
hear,
Words have no words for words that are not
true.

W. H. Auden

The meaning is in the waiting.

R. S. Thomas

Brother Michael SSF

A
Word in
Time

SERMONS AND ADDRESSES

Foreword by
The Right Reverend
LORD RUNCIE

COLT BOOKS
Cambridge

COLT BOOKS LTD
9 Clarendon Road
Cambridge CB2 2BH
tel: 01223 357047 fax: 01223 365866

First published by Colt Books in 1997

Copyright © Michael Fisher SSF 1997

ISBN 0 905899 46 6

Printed in Great Britain by Biddles Ltd, Guildford

CONTENTS

Witnesses to the Word

Addresses

For the Brothers who have lived with me
in Botolph Lane – with love and gratitude

ACKNOWLEDGEMENTS

I would like to express my gratitude to Father Douglas Gale who once again gave his time and imagination to deciphering my writing, producing an accurate manuscript and putting it all on computer. To Dr Elizabeth Walser who generously gives me a safe haven in which to work without disturbance. And to Linda and Robert Yeatman of Colt Books for their unfailing tolerance, encouragement, expertise – and friendship.

NOTE: Quotations from tthe Bible are almost invariably from The New English Bible.

Foreword

by the Right Reverend
LORD RUNCIE

SOMEONE recently appeared in the New Year's Honours List 'For services to the Church of England' and a friend said that it sounded like something on a religious motorway. Not a bad image: and pondering the fast-moving traffic of the last 50 years I decided that few movements had served my church better than the Franciscans. They grew from a brotherhood among the poor of the East End a hundred years ago but have only really taken off in the past fifty. Now they are to be found in San Francisco amidst the casualties of affluence or in Pacific islands among heroic pioneers of the Faith.

Catholic in their roots, evangelical in style, they have evolved a spirituality that is practical rather than other-worldly, which is unpretentious and unpious, which is accessible to all sorts of friends and associates, and which hundreds of people in many lands and many situations have found to be a true path to God and a sure means of serving their neighbour.

Of all this work one of the chief apostles of the 20th century must be Brother Michael. For that reason alone this selection of his sermons and addresses would be of historic value, but there is much more to them than that. The book is not simply an archive.

In presenting us only with addresses and sermons of the last ten years we are receiving the distilled wisdom and experience of fifty. I first met Michael when he appeared as a young Brother in Cambridge in 1949. I was labouring with theological study. Michael made the Word live. I began my ministry in Tyneside where he was a Pied Piper for the young without becoming wholly dependent for his human nourishment on their idolising. This secret explains his survival through all the pressures of priesthood, episcopate, leadership, organisation and world travel. He loves company. New situations spawn fresh enthusiams; but he has never lost that measure of detachment which marked the prayer and discipline of a man of God.

When I asked him to take the Retreat for Bishops of the Anglican Communion in 1988 I had not heard him speak for years; but it was as fresh as it was when he spoke to the young people of Tyneside. If the Church speaks only out of tradition it will end up in speaking only to itself; but if the speaker listens only to the world his views will be a dull echo of the latest fashion. It is the blend of the two which is the genius of the best evangelist and Michael has that. Even so I wondered whether the words of a charismatic presence in the pulpit would be so effective on the printed page. They are. In many ways they are simpler and more assimilable than I remember in his early days (after all he used to read me essays as a pupil at one stage!). It is well worth pondering why this has come about.

Preaching isn't really a trick. It is knowing what you believe and believing it with all your heart and soul. There are some remarks of Arnold Bennett, speaking about literary style but applicable no less to the pulpit or lecture room. "Style cannot be distinguished from matter. When a writer conceives an idea he conceives it in a form of words. That form of words constitutes his style and it is absolutely governed by the idea. The idea, in fact, expresses itself. A clear idea is expressed clearly and a vague idea vaguely. When you know what you think you succeed in saying what you think, in making yourself understood. When you don't know what you think, your expressive tongue halts. And note how in daily life the characteristics of your style follow your mood: how tender it is when you are tender, how violent when you are violent. You have sometimes said to yourself 'If only I could write'. You were wrong.

You ought to have said 'If only I could think and feel'. When you have thought clearly and felt intensely, you have never had any difficulty in saying what you thought, though you may occasionally have had difficulty in keeping it to yourself. When you cannot express yourself, depend upon it you have nothing precise to express, and that what incommodes you is not the vain desire to express yourself better, but the vain desire to think more clearly and to feel more deeply."

The demands from speech over the years for someone so fluent as Michael could have led him into stale garrulity. In fact they seem to have enabled him to speak more clearly and to think more deeply. There are some words written by Owen Chadwick about a hero who is shared by Michael and myself. It was said of Edward King "About the self-discipline there could be no doubt. But what was evident was the humanity, the breadth, the naturalness. Others found in him no tension, no pose, no tautness that he could not relax. . . . To one so gentle they took their problems. And taking them they found in him insight, sympathy and a judgement that illuminated their needs, untied their knots and softened their harshnesses." To encourage the elderly and to inspire the young is what every preacher hopes for. Brother Michael gives us more than a glimpse of how it can be done.

The Rt Revd Lord Runcie
St Albans
January 1997

Introduction

> Prompt me, God;
> But not yet. When I speak,
> Though it be you who speak
> Through me, something is lost.
> The meaning is in the waiting.
>
> *R.S. Thomas*

WHAT'S in a word? For Christians the answer is – a very great deal! The Bible is called "The Word of God" and its stories, poems, wisdom held to be inspired by God. Most sermons are based on a text from the Bible, some verses, even a whole story chosen by the preacher (though as men and women called to preach get to know the Bible very well indeed, it can sometimes seem as if the text chooses them!). They expound or explain the story, explore the ideas, make it relevant to contemporary situations, "rebuke, reprove, exalt", as St Paul says: "Drive the message home." All this and more is the experience of the congregation. For some the sermon *is* the service and can be subject to ruthless criticism.

For the preacher the preparation involves remembering that:

When I speak,

Though it be you who speak

Through me, something is lost.

The meaning is in the waiting.

Waiting on God, waiting for God to tell me what to say. A dangerous business.

And always there is the use of words, remembering that the heart of the Bible is not just a message, but a Man, Jesus, and *He* is called "The Word". "The Word became a human being and lived among us." A living man whose life reflects the very mind of God, and that's what we are talking about when we talk about Him. It is the common theme of all these sermons and addresses.

As that all becomes a personal reality, a personal encounter with Jesus, there can grow a longing to share it, communicate it, just to tell others. It becomes the most powerful incentive in life – and some are called to make it their vocation; a secret you long to reveal, a love you long to share.

There are dangers. A great orator might be a poor preacher, while a man with stumbling words might nevertheless articulate truth in a manner which changes the lives of those who are listening. There *are* techniques in public speaking which can be learnt, and make it easier to convey the message. But at the heart of the matter is the astonishing, humbling and transforming event in the preacher's life of a personal encounter with God in Jesus, through a strength which is not his own but the strength of the Spirit of God. It is nothing to do with particular goodness, worthiness, or any special gift or knowledge, but the mystery – and it *is* a mystery – of knowing that, to quote St Paul, "He loved me, and gave himself for me." He loved me, and I could only respond by loving Him – and from that moment everything else is different.

That recognition not only changes our lives, but changes the way we see the whole world and all that happens in it. Everything. So preachers are always reaching in two directions – towards God and his intention for all creation, and towards the human situation in which we find ourselves. These sermons and addresses do not drag in current events to make them seem "popular" or "up to date"; the events were *already* "in", where we are, where God is speaking to us. The Psalmist says, *"Today* if you will hear His voice harden not your hearts."

They were all given during the past ten years while I was living in Cambridge, as Minister General of the Society of St Francis, and Honorary Assistant Bishop in the Diocese

of Ely. They were written down because there were often
some restrictions of time. Many more were preached from
notes, or were extempore, mostly at Confirmations. I tend-
ed to treat these as Mission Services, of a kind I have
preached in many places, which require a different, more
informal approach and are not easily recorded.

Always there is the question of finding the words. My
mind turns to the things that are happening all round me,
and my concerns come to the surface; Health and
Wholeness: Peace (I found the Gulf War a great challenge):
Death and Bereavement: the witness of other women and
men: the Religious Orders. Even more important, the
humanity of God, His compassion and love and the way He
draws us all into His divinity by sharing it with us. The
mystery of human love in all its wonder, and the power of
forgiveness when we misuse it. Jesus as Saviour.

All this defies words, unless we recognise that preachers
and poets have this in common, that they dare to say things
that are almost beyond words – and it's dangerous ground!
"Words have no words for words which are not true." It is
easy to talk about love, increasingly difficult to put our
growing awareness of all it means into words. As much is
true of the wonder and glory of God and that eternal life
with Him, which is the greater reality.

So we wait, and sometimes a sermon comes to mind
more or less complete and only needs to be written down.
At other times the waiting is prolonged and when it comes
can be laborious, word upon word: and sometimes these
seem the best as we discover that the meaning *is* in the
waiting; something given by God.

St Bene't's (St Benedict's) is the church in the centre of
Cambridge with a Saxon tower. A thousand years old, it is
a holy place, which conveys a sense of being "set apart" for
prayer. Anglican Franciscan Brothers have been Vicars for
fifty years. I celebrated the Eucharist there for the first time
in 1953. It is a good place in which to preach. The pulpit is

right among the congregation, who listen carefully, and can be constructively critical.

Ely is the Cathedral in which I was ordained Deacon and Priest, and it was a great privilege to be welcomed as Assistant Bishop. Its beauty and the marvellous symmetry of its great Norman nave – surely one of the finest in Europe – never fails to excite in me a sense of awe and wonder.

I preached several times at about the time of the Gulf War. First at Sandringham where the Queen and members of the Royal family gather at Christmas, and she is in residence for eight weeks. A bishop is invited to stay each weekend, and preach at Mattins on the Sunday morning. The church is small, and the Royal family and their guests take up the whole of the chancel. There is however a very large congregation – sometimes thousands – who drive over and hear the service relayed while they sit in their cars. So for several reasons it is a rather unusual opportunity. The following Sunday I was at Oundle School. Intending to share some of my feelings at the outbreak of World War II I was surprised to discover that no-one, from the Headmaster down, was old enough to remember it!

The first Music Festival at which I was invited to preach was for the opening service of the Three Choirs in Hereford. Brecon Jazz Festival is different. I preached in a packed Cathedral at the inaugural service of the first one, supported by a Big Band from America, and a Marching Band from Holland, and returned ten years later taking a text from George Gershwin's *Porgy and Bess*. It is one of the great annual festivals. The whole town is closed: there are bands everywhere – a really great Jazz occasion.

Edinburgh speaks for itself. I have long known the Episcopal Cathedral and, as in some other places, there is for me a sense of homecoming.

Much of my ministry has been in the student world, and theological colleges in particular. Returning to Cambridge gave me an opportunity to renew a ministry which is always a privilege, and some of the addresses here reflect that.

I am also deeply aware of the tradition into which we are called: and these talks acknowledge my commitment to the Religious Life, and some particular people whose goodness and holiness are an inspiration to me.

Franciscans, like other Religious, are frequently invited to take, or lead, "Retreats" – groups of people who spend a period of time (often three or four days) in silence to pray together and allow God to enter their lives and help them. The leader, or conductor as he is sometimes called, is there to generally guide and help them individually or corporately. Sometimes he gives addresses on a theme. The retreat addresses included here were given in the Chapel of Lambeth Palace for all the Primates of the Anglican Communion before the Lambeth Conference. I had used the theme of 2 Timothy before on many occasions, and had become very familiar with this little Epistle, and have never failed to be led to something new in it. That particular retreat was the source of very real blessing for me, and I have looked back on it with gratitude. I subsequently made it the basis for retreats in America; for all the clergy of the Diocese of Rhode Island and then for the clergy of the Diocese of St Louis, Missouri.

One of the strange but wonderful things about preaching is that though there is, generally speaking, no way of measuring what it has done for others (immediate impressions one way or another can be very misleading) I can only be humbly thankful to God for the way in which, through this particular ministry, He has continued to make Himself known to me and been a channel for His friendship in the family of His Love.

Sermons in St Bene't's Church, Cambridge

Waiting on God

Be strong and of good courage. Keep alert
with all perseverance.   *Josh 1:1-9*

T HERE is a poem by R. S. Thomas, which might be
regarded as a warning to preachers. He says:

Moments of great calm
Kneeling before an altar
Of wood in a stone church
In summer, waiting for God
To speak:
        All that close throng
Of Spirits waiting, as I,
For the message.
        Prompt me God
But not yet. When I speak
Though it be you who speak
Through me, something is lost.
The meaning is in the waiting.

Well, it is summer, under the cloths the altar in this church
is of wood, and these ancient stones have stood for a thousand years of waiting. Waiting for God to speak – and
waiting for us. So we also come here Sunday by Sunday
waiting for God to speak – though much of the time we
crowd Him out with words. So much information given to
God who knows it all, and has known it all from time and
for eternity. Church can become a place of impatience.

Dare we even call His name? Thomas has another poem
he just calls *Waiting*:

Young, I pronounced you, older
I still do, but seldomer.
Now, leaning far out,

Over an immense depth letting
Your name go and waiting
Somewhere between faith and doubt
For the echo of its arrival.

How much of life is taken up in waiting. Waiting as children for a holiday, or a party. Oh the intolerable tedium of time that passes so slowly – ticking off the days, or waiting with fear, for examination results. The "suppressed" tension of a household expecting the news of A-levels or Finals.

How far can nine months stretch when a baby is to be born; or waiting for the medical verdict that indicates the extension or the termination of this life. Waiting can so easily become just a terrible emptiness between events, a deadland.

Nothing speaks so eloquently of the possibility of wasted space in life than the ubiquitous waiting room – doctors, dentists, opticians, offices: "I hope you don't mind waiting," "Sorry to keep you waiting," "I'm afraid you'll have to wait – no I can't tell you for how long." Empty hours on benches, in an unnatural silence of shared fear, or anxiety, even dread. Speaking in whispers. I wouldn't be surprised if the average man or woman spends more time in waiting than sleeping.

By contrast, one of the most discerning books on the spiritual life, by Hubert Vanstone, is called *The Stature of Waiting*. He suggests that this power of waiting was an essential characteristic of Jesus – and that in His waiting, He permitted the disclosure of God to us – "leaning far out, letting His name go, waiting, somewhere between faith and doubt, for the echo of its arrival". What is true for Him is true for us – made in His image. Vanstone says, "To man, as he waits, the world discloses its power of meaning. Man becomes, so to speak, the sharer with God of a secret – the secret of the world's power of meaning."

Perhaps the meaning *can* lie in the waiting, a waiting that is filled not with emptiness but with everything. There is a Benedictine nun who was for many years the Abbess of the convent in which she has lived all her life since she went there as a girl – and now she is over ninety. Two weeks ago she was told she has an inoperable cancer. When someone tried to comfort her she replied: "But darling I've got to die of *something*, and there is still so much I can do." All her life, waiting on God - great stretches of silence, dropping God's name – waiting for the echo. An echo that is reflected repeatedly in the psalms: "My soul truly waiteth still upon God for of Him cometh my salvation". So for her it has been seventy years of waiting in that one convent and finding it an anteroom of heaven.

But you might say either: "What an awful waste", or "In any case that is her vocation. God called her – she's a long way from where we are, well away from the nitty gritty." The testimony of such women down the ages is of something very different. It seems that if we are ever to understand the stature of waiting, our involvement in the meaning of the world, we need to turn to just such a woman and such a place: and of this we are reminded in the scripture. Again and again in the Old Testament we are challenged: "Be strong and of good courage." Why? For the people of Israel everything was coming good. All those countless years of waiting in the wilderness, and now for them (as you might say also for the holy nun) the goal was in sight. The promised land. For Moses, a hope only, but for Joshua and the whole tribe a reality. Home at last. Now says God, the reality is at hand – the true conflict.

And St Paul is no less certain: "Be strong in the Lord - put on your armour, and wait upon God – having done all to *stand*." Are you waiting? Then, says St Paul, keep alert. This is no time for empty nothingness – rather a time for growing in strength. And he details the armour needed to fight. (*Ephesians 6: 11-17*)

Only if we are truly waiting still upon God, do we begin to recognise the power of evil in the world. The appalling

11

truth is that when God came Himself into the world, waiting to reveal Himself in Jesus, the whole time of waiting
was one of warfare – not just resisting temptation, though
there was that, but having done all to stand. Standing firm
– recognising the true enemy. "For we fight, as he did, not
against flesh and blood but against spiritual wickedness."
It can be lonely waiting. "The disciples all forsook him and
fled." Remember, we see Him in the light of the resurrection – the disciples hadn't that advantage, and neither have
the majority of the good honest pagans in the world, both
inside as well as outside the Church.

Waiting can be lonely. All those failed assignations: "I'll
meet you under the clock." So in the Christian life, the
Spiritual life. We can wait, and it seems, He didn't turn up.
We know about the clock. The time dragging past – where
was He, where *is* He? No wonder our friends find us odd,
that we still persist.

Eliot says in *East Coker*:

> I said to my soul be still and wait
> > without hope
> For hope would be hope for the wrong thing
> > wait without love
> For love would be love of the wrong thing:
> > there is yet faith
> But the faith, the hope and the love are
> > All in the waiting.

So Jesus prayed in the Gospel, "protect them from the
evil one" – that is, protect you and me: and St Paul encourages us to protection, using an image of soldiers and warfare. Well the English, not to mention the Anglicans, love a
military metaphor, and sometimes as a result miss the
point. It is not just another way of saying "Onward
Christian Soldiers". This warfare will take you with Jesus
to the lonely waiting in the wilderness and perhaps to an
encounter with the devil himself; or to Gethsemane and
face to face with God; or even to the wonder and the doubt

of an empty tomb. And to face that St Paul says, "Above all take the shield of faith with which you can face all the flaming darts of the evil one."

As you wait upon God so you will really grow in stature, discovering that the faith, the love and the hope are all in the waiting. But the reward is of sometimes hearing, as if for the first time, the true echo of His Voice in your heart – and from Him comes your salvation.

Children of His Love
A CHRISTMAS SERMON

You will conceive in the womb and bear a
Son and shall call his name Jesus.   *Luke 1:31*

THERE are two poems by T. S. Eliot which remind us
of childbirth and Christmas. In one he says:

Issues from the hand of God the simple soul
To a flat world of changing lights and noise,
To light, dark, dry or damp, chilly or warm;
Moving between the legs of tables and of chairs,
Rising or falling, sudden to take alarm,
Retreating to the corner of arm and knee,
Eager to be reassured, taking pleasure
In the fragrant brilliance of the Christmas tree.

Amazing that the apparently dry old poet can so exactly
capture the tentative exploring world of a little child. Any
child, the child perhaps, those words bring to your mind.

Yes, but among the children it brings to my mind is one
I saw pictured in *The Times* a week or two ago. A lovely boy
in his mother's arms, chubby and cheerful, born to a flat
world of light and dark. And the dark for him is that he is
a victim of the AIDS virus – given him by his mother, who
was infected perhaps by his father.

There is always a crisis at Christmas for some children -
born into a world of "dry or damp, chilly or warm", as
Eliot says, a world of terrible and inadequate housing, of
battered babies, the Esther Rantzen world of cruel violence.
And now this Christmas there is something new.

Of course we've faced it all before, been indignant,
protested, raised money, written letters, held meetings. Yet
our memories can be short. Do you remember Biafra? What

14

happened to the babies of Biafra? And Chernobyl – what about the children of Chernobyl? Ethiopia - *did* Bob Geldof put it all right for us? There are always babies in Beirut – and for that matter in Belfast as well.

Of every case, every single one, Eliot says:

Issues from the hand of God the simple soul.

From the hand of God; the unsuspecting, innocent, help-less, vulnerable, fragile soul and body of a baby. That is what happened to each one of them and each one of us. I have no idea what privations, deprivations, rejections, you may have suffered as a child, or the degree to which your mother was exposed to suffering on your behalf. Our birth is itself a crisis, an event which changes the world, and from the moment we are conceived, the world changes us. But we too issued from the hand of God.

We are asked today to recall with gratitude an event which, in spite of theological controversy, all would agree is unique. The announcing of another conception. Be doubtful of angels if you wish – to me they make a lot of sense. The important thing to note, as indeed the Gospel declares, is that, to use a colloquialism, Mary got the mes-sage. A baby would be born, and she would be the mother – and his name would be Jesus, that, as St Matthew points out, means Saviour. And more than that, his name will be Emmanuel, meaning: "God is with us". So "issues from the hand of God the simple soul" – a brown Israel/Arab baby. God from the hand of God. Or as we say: "God of God, Light of light, Very God of Very God, begotten not made, of one being with the Father by whom all things were made."

What God his father transmitted to Mary, what she trans-mitted to her Son, was the grace and light and glory of Godhead, the divinity which is eternal.

Yet all held in the fragile, vulnerable flesh which is yours and mine, the battered baby's and the broken bodies, the bruised, the starving, those who will die while this sermon

15

is being preached, as well as the beautiful, the bouncing, the bonny.

John Donne, preaching in St Paul's Cathedral on Christmas Day in 1625 said:

> How much misery is presaged for us when we come so generally weeping into this world . . . What miserable revolutions and changes, what downfalls, what break necks and precipitations . . . Yet, only to Jesus the fullness of time was at His birth; not because he also had not a painful life to pass through, but because the work of our redemption was an entire work, and all that Christ said or did or suffered, concurred to our salvation; as well his mother's swathing him in little clouts as Joseph's shrouding him in a funerall sheete.

Can we take in the wonder that Mary the Mother of Jesus should be so completely one with the vulnerable world of motherhood – the misunderstanding, the stigma of illegitimacy, the narrow escape from slaughter, the refugee flight to Egypt. What does it do to the mothers of the world, bringing children into political conflict – the sudden rap on the door, the firing squads, the detention centre, the vast camps for homeless wanderers on the face of the earth? The compassion of Mary for the mothers of the world is reflected in the promise to her: "a sword shall pierce through your heart also".

The Annunciation is also a proclamation, a challenge, a banner, a demonstration, a cry from the heart of God to the heart of men. The meek Mary is also the challenging woman of liberation: "He has put down the mighty, exalted the humble, fed the hungry, sent away the rich – empty".

Forget for a moment the misplaced power of men; the fantasy of security which can squander a billion pounds on Nimrod, fight futile political wars, deny freedom to women and men for no other reason but the colour of their skin. The misplaced power of men can lead only, as Donne said, to "shrouding in a funeral sheet". Think only that this

16

SERMONS IN ST BENE'T'S CHURCH

Christmas we celebrate the divine intervention, the exaltation of mothers, and find in the children – all the children – the compelling power of love, the new humanity which might yet change our own hearts and lives. "Except you change and become as a little child", said Jesus, "you cannot enter the Kingdom of Heaven."

"Except ye be converted," the old translation said. Shall we reserve conversion only for our preaching of the Cross? Cannot mankind be changed at Christmas? The prophet says, "A little child shall lead them." The Christ Child, Mary's Child – any child might lead you to change your life – retreating to the corner of arm or knee, the safety of arms, that in their trusting life, are everlasting arms no matter how unworthy I may feel.

Change in a way which will make a demand on your priorities in life, your scale of values, shake you from lethargy or complacency to action, lead you to believe in yourself, and the part you can play in making the world a place where the initiative of God who brings the children into the world is matched by the initiative of man making it a place where the children may not merely survive but live creatively to God's glory as citizens of the Kingdom of Heaven. Rejoice if you like in the fragrant brilliance of the Christmas tree – but rejoice even more, infinitely more, in the fragrant brilliance of Childhood.

And decide that you have indeed to become as a little child and give your own heart to God. Be born again.

I said I would mention two poems by Eliot. The second is one which it has been suggested might chronicle Eliot's own conversion – *The Journey of the Magi*, the three wise men. It concludes:

> This set down
> This, were we led all that way for
> Birth or Death? There was a birth certainly,
> We had evidence and no doubt. I had seen birth and
>   death

17

But had thought they were different: this Birth was
Hard and bitter agony for us, like death our death
We returned to our places, Mere kingdoms
But no longer at ease here in the old dispensation,
With an alien people clutching their Gods
I should be glad of another death.

This Christmas we might not only celebrate a child's birth but the death of our old self, perhaps never again to be at ease in the tinsel world of make-believe, but all the more rejoicing with the angels that a King has been born into the Heaven of this world, and made us children of His love.

Turning Charity into Love

And now abideth faith hope and charity,
these three: but the greatest of these is
charity.   *1 Cor 13:13*

J UST four years ago a friend died in a London hospital
of AIDS (or more strictly he died of illnesses which his
body could not cope with because his immune system had
been destroyed by AIDS).

A small group of his closest friends agreed that there
would always be two of them with him night and day. The
hospital was crowded, the nurses hard-pressed. So they
were able to help with some basic nursing, and were with
him when he died, only six days later.

Because of this sad anniversary I found I could not avoid
asking myself the question: what does this say to me about
Faith and Charity?

The answer must depend in the first place on what I
believe my Faith to be. I'll try to be brief.

When I am challenged I know in my heart that it makes
more sense for me to believe in a world entirely made and
sustained by God. That He created everything including
me. And that in spite of horrific aeroplane crashes,
appalling diseases and devastating earthquakes, causing so
much human suffering, He is a God of love who invites us
to call him Father, a personal God who sees us as part of the
family of Man, made in His image, to be like Him and share
His life.

I also believe – and sometimes it seems an awful lot to
believe – that far greater than my faith in Him is *His* faith
in me. He didn't stay away out there, away from the crashes, diseases and disasters, but He came right here. In Jesus
we see God sharing the humanity He made. This surely is

19

the most important thing we ever have to learn and know in our hearts as well as our heads. In Jesus we see the Divinity of God. In Jesus we see also the humanity of God. And because it is in Him, it is in you and me as well. This is no new discovery, it has always been there. You don't get it by going to Church, being holy or becoming a clergyman. It is the way God designed things from the start and Jesus came to wake us up to the fact. Some people seem to wake up almost too much and put on so much artificial divinity that it puts other people off! Others get so hooked on the humanity they try to manage without God, and wonder why it doesn't quite work. Only Jesus got it absolutely right – and died in the doing of it! So much for faith. What about Charity?

I was struck again by the absolute wonder of St Paul's great song in Corinthians from which I have taken my text. "Though I give all my goods to feed the poor and have not Charity it profiteth me nothing." But surely that is what Charity is – giving to the poor, and the sick and the homeless and hungry as well. I am sure you are genuinely good about that in giving to Oxfam, War on Want, Barnardos, The Wishing Well and all the other recognised charities, and I hope with all my heart you will continue to do so.

In any case, someone by now will, I am sure, want to remind me that all the recent translations say *Love*, and not Charity, quite rightly. Then when, or how, does Charity become Love?

There is a true story of Jesus in St Mark's Gospel about a leper who came to Jesus and said: "If you will you can make me clean". In warm indignation Jesus replied, "I will, *be* clean. And stretching out his hand he touched him. Lepers were treated in the time of Jesus as TB patients were treated when I was a boy, and AIDS patients are often treated now. "Untouchable" is the word. Jesus *touched* him, and Charity became Love. He didn't just heal him in charity – he *joined* him in love, said "we have a common humanity", made himself ceremonially unclean with him.

20

Francis of Assisi, 700 years ago, faced with a leper did the same thing. He was going to offer him money – but on impulse threw his arms round him and kissed him. It was the beginning of new life for both of them.

We are all here this morning, whether we realise it or not, because we have felt the touch of Jesus. You know your needs as I know mine, sickness, disappointment, failure, the disasters or fears you brought with you, joys and happiness as well, I hope. How often in our loneliness have we said: "Please don't touch me"? Did you come for Charity? In Charity He can heal you – in Love He will join you. And because that is a principle of His life, it should be a principle in yours and mine.

So what do I do about the boy of sixteen who stood in front of me on a crowded platform in the underground at Charing Cross a few weeks ago and said in a broad northern accent: "I'm out of work, homeless and hungry" – and held out his hand. Give him money – that's Charity. But touch him? To do *that*, if I'm serious I have to take on board the whole question of homes in the industrial wastelands of the north, broken by despair, of lads who leave school knowing there's no job to go to, of overcrowded schools, overworked social workers. To touch him I have to believe I can touch politicians and the educational system, just as much as I need to touch the Health Service if we are to have the facilities to face an AIDS epidemic; or the various services in London who might save that same boy from becoming a prostitute and a new agent for spreading of that same disease – in such ways do social problems feed on one another.

Jesus always challenged the rich – and there is a sickness of affluence that needs his touch. A sickness in society that encourages the rapid acquisition of unearned wealth in the hands of the comparatively few that distorts the values of the many and renders us vulnerable to innate selfishness. A sickness at Sotheby's – where one or two Van Goghs could buy all the CAT Scans and kidney machines we want, and give health and hope to many, many people. There are many charities that command our compassion – and you will see their ads in today's Sunday papers – the MS Society, the cancer societies, Mind, and so on. AIDS seems to serve the greater need as reflecting an even wider vulnerability, and in Charity – you can give to the Terrence Higgins Trust, the London Lighthouse and others who will be glad of your money. But how will you translate your Charity into Love? My friend who died only four years ago, was about the fiftieth person to die from an AIDS related sickness. Already in that short time the figure is now over a thousand – and still rising. A conservative estimate suggests that there are now more than 50,000 persons carrying the virus in this country.

In spite of widespread campaigns, I find intelligent people still remarkably ill-informed; young people who insist, "It couldn't happen to me".

With our new affluence it is just easier to give Charity than overcome our prejudice, pride, our shyness, diffidence, embarrassment or just plain fear and say – out loud – "You are made in the image of God – the humanity of Jesus is in you – the dignity, beauty and delight of Love is worth the discipline of life that is the one thing that can prevent the spread of AIDS – but, more positively, can give you a richer, more joyful and fulfilled life than you could ever imagine – because it will bring you close to God!"

All right – so they'd run a mile or give a mocking laugh to *those* words. Then find the words that will fit the occasion. Remember the warm indignation of Jesus, and the kiss of Francis, and learn by faith how to turn Charity into Love, how to touch others as Christ has touched you.

The Violence of Love

Ever since the coming of John the Baptist
the Kingdom of Heaven has been subjected
to violence.   *Matt 11:2-15*

T HE two boys were, of course, cousins. Their mothers
were not only related but intimate friends. So to begin
with we might imagine that they too were friends, shared
their ideas and were not, I hope, always serious. I'm talking, of course, of Jesus and John, the John who later was
called the Baptist. But it didn't last. John was the wild one,
going off into the desert, dressing like a prophet, living
rough, regarded by some, no doubt, as mad, and by others
as dangerous, while Jesus became "the Carpenter's Son" –
about his father's business, the good boy who stayed at
home. In spite of his wildness, as the time passed John
attracted followers, disciples, converts. Membership rites
included deliberate plunging into water – which is how he
got his name of Baptist. Above all he had a message, he was
the herald of a new age, a new way of looking at the whole
of human life, the whole of creation. It was called "The
Kingdom".

Jesus too eventually became restless and left home. Some
think that like his cousin he disappeared into the desert, to
live for years in a sort of monastery near the Dead Sea –
until such time as he was ready to take up his ministry.

When he did so, it was, like John, to attract disciples who
could not resist the message, or the man. And it was the
same message, "The Kingdom of Heaven is at hand". And
these two men, Jesus and John, changed the world, for ever.
To appreciate the impact of their message it is necessary
always to remember two things. Firstly, in the time of Jesus
the Jewish faith and the practice of it dominated the whole

23

of life, absolutely everything. How you ate, slept, protested, washed, worked, as well as how you prayed. It dominated all human relationships, put everyone in their place from the leper to the lord. It was an inflexible and unquestioned structure, dominated by the Rabbis and ruled by the Pharisees.

Jesus challenged it all – from top to bottom – and John knew he would. His manifesto was largely lifted from the writing of the Jewish Prophets – which made the Pharisees mad – no-one likes their own texts being thrown back to them.

So, secondly, the message was revolutionary: "The blind receive their sight, the lame walk, the lepers are made clean, the deaf hear, the dead are raised to life, the poor are hearing the Good News."

And because that implied far more than physical blindness or deafness or lameness, because Jesus came to reverse all the merely worldly values it brought him, as it had already brought John, into conflict with the authorities.

There is a terrible picture by Aubrey Beardsley, one of his illustrations for Oscar Wilde's play *Salome* – a long hairy arm holds aloft a large plate dripping blood with the staring head of John the Baptist on it. The consequence of preaching the Kingdom for both the boys was a violent death.

So this difficult text begins to come alive. "Ever since John the Baptist the Kingdom of Heaven has been subject to violence." Is there a paradox here? Surely the whole point of the Kingdom is Peace. And for those who bravely and consistently pursue the path of peaceful non-violence, as Gandhi did, I have the most sincere admiration, indeed I have their ideal. They do see the Kingdom come. Yet hard in the wake of Independence in India were some of the most terrible massacres of this century.

For some our text might mean: "The Kingdom of heaven suffers violence. And men of violence grab it." Others would say it means: "The Kingdom of Heaven manifests

24

itself violently and daring men take hold of it." Jesus the daring Man, a very different thing. And, you might say, do such fine points of interpretation matter today? Well, we, the Christian community, are still in the business of making the Kingdom of Heaven known in a sometimes hostile world. If you take it seriously then you will find yourself confronted with violence in one way or another, sometimes other people's, sometimes your own.

During the past week there have been three major news items, all related to violence. It may seem trivial compared with other things, but for the Captain of the English team to swear at the umpire and refuse to accept his ruling was just not Cricket. The worst day, we were told, in the history of the game. It's the tip of another iceberg in the breakdown of human relationship. In the same week a football hooligan was put in prison for eight years. A week ago a boxer attacked the referee. Men who in competition once represented the finer side of all our lives now represent something violent, acquisitive, hostile.

Secondly, for all of us, inside and outside the Church, the sad death by his own hand of Canon Garry Bennett seemed infinitely more significant. For here is violence inside the Church. As Cricket has always been dependent in the past on a gentlemen's agreement that you never question the decision of the umpire, so the Church of England has grown to suppose that similar sorts of rules apply. You could trust in the idea of an anonymous preface to *Crockford's Clerical Directory* because the writer, who is "one of us", would know where to draw the line. But suppose you overlook the pressures of the world from which the Kingdom of Heaven suffers violence. Garry Bennett was not the only one who believed that this violence is attacking the very life and integrity of the Church of England. Perhaps he was wrong in his views – he seems to have died for them. The violence found its way into the body of Christ – and we all suffer. The media have a field day focusing it all on the Archbishop, who deserves our sympathy, love and prayerful support – but it's not the real point. *That* lies in a deeper awareness and understanding of responsibility the Church has to proclaim the Kingdom, and when it has a divided voice – as it has at present – to be humble as it discovers a way of reconciliation.

And thirdly there was the Summit. A clear step back from the brink. One step on a long march. But not from Aldermaston. That seems to be over. To me it seemed a little distant and unreal, all the razzmatazz in Washington. And then I heard the word Greenham, and I remembered a distinguished clerical friend of mine apologising for the absence of his daughter – because she was at Greenham Common. And it brought home to me the modest violence of those persistent women. And now the missiles will eventually go. But the violence won't.

How can we, practically, spiritually speaking meet that – the violence creeping into every part of life from child abuse to football teams, into the Church, into the world. Well there is one way.

Jesus, the daring Man, dared all and died the victim of violence. Characteristically he met violence with violence – the violence of absolute love, a violence that may yet seize the Kingdom of Heaven on earth.

The message of John the Baptist was, after all, "*Repent,* for the Kingdom of Heaven is at hand" and let's face it, if you take it seriously, there's nothing more violent than that.

On Being Angry with God

What right have you, a human being, to cross-question God?

I N the past few days I have been visiting a young woman who is very angry. She is only twenty-eight. Four years ago she had a transplant of her heart and both her lungs – a remarkable operation, involving an enormous resource of medical and surgical skill, nursing dedication and quite considerable logistical expertise; after all, a very sick patient, the donor's heart and lungs, the hospital staff and medical team, all had to be brought together very quickly for an operation that costs thousands of pounds. It was very successful. Within two years she was living a perfectly normal, happy married life. And now, infection, rejection; treatment so new that it is in a sense experimental; and all the happiness threatened by the imminent prospect of death. So was it all in vain? She says: "I am very angry with God. What is He up to? It's surely such an unfair world. I can't trust Him any more."

I could say, in the words of my text: "What right have you to cross-question God?"

She is the third woman I have sat with in Papworth Hospital during the past year, all in the same position with cystic fibrosis – and all only about thirty years old. One of them, Emma, is already dead. In the small world of those who have had this astonishing operation, Emma is particularly remembered. We talked about her. Her radiance, her assurance, her ability to minister to her husband and everyone who felt unable to face what was to happen. It was no surprise, but a sort of reassurance that not long before the final onslaught she had been ordained Deacon.

To be angry or not to be angry? Emma wasn't angry.

27

There is, after all, so much in the world about which we might justifiably feel angry – really cross-question God. Why *do* you permit this? What is it about your love that it seems only to triumph in the face of adversity, can never be taken at its face value?

It is a question which has been asked from the beginning of man's awareness of the possibility of some supernatural Being who represents the origin of all things, the mind behind the creation, its purpose and the power that sustains it. The Jews personalised it and called it God. Later they discovered they had not been wrong, but thought that the One God whom they finally recognised and worshipped was a God to be feared – whose justice could act with ruthless ferocity, particularly against those who misguidedly challenged, ignored or defied him. Yet he was such a God as never entirely destroyed in justice or retribution. Their story of Noah was the result. God says: "I wish I hadn't made them. I'll destroy the lot of them,"and then, "No, I'll save a few, give them another start." So the ark, and the animals, human and otherwise, went in two by two. And at the end of the flood, a rainbow – and he said "Pax", and they all made a Covenant – and promised to be good.

That was myth – but history proved otherwise. In Egypt the Jews had an awful time – it ended with the slaughter of the baby boys. But God still determined to save something from it all – so we have another story, of Moses, the baby in the bulrushes. And it goes on. Of course they *did* cross-question God again and again. There were fresh disasters up to the biggest one of all – the conquest, the destruction of Jerusalem, the death of the King – and the Captivity. And in captivity the Psalmist says: "Why hast thou so dealt with us?" "Why is your wrath so hot against your people, the sheep of your pasture, what have we done to deserve it?" After seventy years, under a friendly ruler, there is once more a remnant to return and rebuild Jerusalem. But though they didn't know it, and wouldn't listen to the few who did, they were paving the way for the ultimate remnant. One man, and even he, like Moses, was saved in childhood when all his contemporaries, the other little baby boys, were killed by Herod.

And this remnant, this one Man, Christ Jesus – he died *young* questioning God, saying like the girl in the hospital, "Why have you forsaken me?" So he died – as she will. As indeed we all will, only not necessarily in the quiet certainty of old age like a saintly Simeon, departing in peace – but in the prime of life and promise as He did. But there is a difference far more profound. "There is a new covenant", he says, "in my blood." "My death will make sense of all death, will answer your anger – and all your questions. But only a remnant will understand. You will have to think as I think, see things from my point of view, see them from the height of the cross and the perspective of heaven."

"Many will appear to follow me, be my Church, a new Israel, but even there only a remnant will really understand."

Of the rest, many will be disappointed, fall away, say there is nothing here for me. And it won't take much – a cold church or a hymn you don't like or can't sing; rivalry in the congregation or a social, political or theological opinion that doesn't fit, the erosion of apathy or the attraction of other ways of seeing things, the inexplicable paradoxes of the Christian Faith; or just personal pique, perhaps most of all the necessity of being in a minority that can seem a collection of cranks. After all, I wonder what the neighbours thought of Noah!

I think God understands our anger. He was angry too. Sometimes anger is the only form of love that can meet a situation. The anger of love also seems a bit of a paradox. That is why we cross-question God. "Why have you forsaken *me*? And the children in Yugoslavia suffering in a civil war, and the babies born with AIDS in Central Africa? How can the Irish kill each other in the name of Christ? What sort of cross-questioning is that? And why should

Emma die when she had just dedicated herself as your servant in the Body of your Son which is the Church?" We all have our own agenda of anger.

And the answer is in the body of His Son on the cross who not only said: "Why have you forsaken me?" but "Father, forgive them" and inaugurated a new covenant in His Blood. It is His sons and daughters, those who persist in living by that covenant in spite of all, who can share their anger with Him, argue their cause with Him, and finally triumph over suffering and death with Him. It hasn't much to do with ecclesiastical organisation – but everything to do with life eternal. Perhaps only a remnant discover that, though it is open to all to know. But the next time you have a grudge against God and take it to Him, even in anger, you may discover that you are in fact a part of the remnant, after all, and looking up recognise blazing in all its beauty, as Noah did, the Bow in the Cloud.

It Has Been Granted to You . . .

It has been granted to you to know the
secrets of the Kingdom of God.   *Luke 8:10*

Preached during a University Mission led by
Jean Vanier, Sheila Cassidy and Bishop David Jenkins

T HE news last Sunday seemed dominated for me by the
death of Brian Redhead – and so was the news on
Radio 4 the following morning in a programme, *Today*,
which he had made his own for so many years. But that
was not the only death to be mourned by a nation – the
other was that of Sir Matt Busby, the Grand Old Man of
English football. The shock of Brian's death was com-
pounded by his early age, he was only sixty-four, but the
shock was no less great at Matt's, though he was eighty-
four. Thousands lined the streets at his funeral and the
Roman Catholic Bishop of Salford spoke of his magical
powers and great humility: that his life was one of healing
and inspiration; of challenge renewed. He never abandoned a devout Catholicism, never exploited celebrity, felt
no restraint in decorum, was a working class hero of cour-
tesy, and a gentleman.

Both he and Brian Redhead had a faith refined in the
crucible of suffering. Matt Busby was in the same plane
which in February 1958 crashed, killing eight of his young
players – "Busby's Babes" – whom he regarded with
unqualified affection and pride as his sons. And Brian
learned of that suffering of love when his own son was
killed at the age of eighteen in a car crash. For them both it
was a turning point in depth and understanding of their
faith in God.

They were both great communicators. For Matt Busby

31

football was his life. Not the crude thuggery that sometimes creeps into the current game – but the sheer artistry,
finesse and beauty of the game at its best – and which he
wanted everyone to share. And as to Brian – the unselfish
exuberance of a man who lent his entire life to be as
informed as he could be, and then exercising his exceptional skills in making it available to others in radio,
television, books, making you feel he was always just
talking to you, as of course he was. Was either of them ever
maddening? Undoubtedly, after all they were human, very
human. But something of the image of God shone through
them, and the distinct and different personalities they were
– which can be true of us all.

I don't know if Matt Busby ever wanted to be a priest.
Brian Redhead did seriously think about it – and was
advised to give up the idea – it would spoil it all to cleri-
calise him. And so it would! Well, you don't have to be a
priest to preach the Gospel – which brings me at last to
today's sermon - *Jesus' teaching*. The story of the sower: a
parable taken from the familiar world of the countryside.

There is another account of the same parable in St Mark
– indeed they may have both copied it from the same
source, but Mark helps us by putting in more detail,
perhaps he was there, heard it himself at the time. The picture is of quite a large crowd who had gathered to hear
him. He needs more room. It is Mark who tells us he was
by the lake of Galilee, and that he got into a boat - Peter's
or John's, who knows? – that they pushed him away from
the shore, and he sat there, found space, and the crowds
pressed forward on the beach, right down to the water's
edge – another bit of personal observation.

As to the parable, it seems fairly obvious. The sower
sowing seeds, carrying a large tray, taking handfuls, and
skilfully throwing them in a wide arc around him. It is still
done in some parts of the world like that – and it is sur-
prising how evenly it seems to fall – but on hard ground,
stony ground, footpaths, among weeds, as well as on good

ground. The ground was then immediately ploughed and the seeds as well, with a wooden plough, by hand, or with an ox. I've seen that too. And with all the inevitable consequences.

But of course it was the interpretation of the parable that counted.

To the crowd Jesus cries out, "If you have ears to hear then hear." But the disciples, who I assume had crowded into the boat with him – sitting on the platform with him as it were - say, "Please interpret this for us". Well, we all know what can happen to even the simplest message, like, shall we say, "Back to Basics" – which it seems no-one can interpret!

In this case it is far more serious, and in a sense, basic matter.

What we must never lose sight of in all the teaching of Jesus is that *His* fundamental and basic message is contained in the words "the Kingdom". So he says here, "It has been granted to you to know the secrets of the Kingdom of God." And the others, well sadly, "they look and see nothing, hear and understand nothing." *That's* the message – *recognising the Kingdom.* Ever since Jesus was in the world the Kingdom has been, as it were, coming at us, being taught us by Jesus, the Word made flesh and living among us. And the explanation of the parable is a dramatic explanation of just what happens. When the word *does* get through the results can be dramatic, just think of Jean Vanier and Sheila Cassidy last week during the University Mission - not to mention the Bishop of Durham, David Jenkins, though he can be suspect because he's a professional, a bishop.

Jesus wasn't addressing the professionals, in fact, it was the professional clerics of his time, the Scribes and Pharisees, who were the very ones who were blind and deaf to the message of the Kingdom, shocked by his parables, infuriated by miracles, and who finally turned to the ultimate censorship by killing the teacher. But it was too late, the word had got out – to the men in the boat.

The seed, says Jesus, is the Word of God. And the message is the Man, the Man who taught us to pray "Thy Kingdom come on earth". Hearing the message is not easy, understanding and accepting it harder still. The rich young man thought he'd heard it – but departed in sorrow because he was rich, and preferred that. Many hear it in their early teens, but the message gets trampled under the feet of those whose expectations are of power or success for its own sake. For others it is sadly not choked by the outside world so much as by the bewildering world of religion, with its division, back-biting, envy, fear, jealousy, or its sheer boredom. For others it seems to involve too much pain, too little joy – and that's the biggest tragedy in some ways, because in reality the very reverse is the case. Not that it is without pain, but there is pain for everyone, suffering, and ultimately death. Remember, the messenger also had to die. But he died in order to demonstrate his own solidarity with us all, people who are preparing for death by living the life of the Kingdom on earth. And that involves starting all over again.

Jesus said: "Unless you become" – at any age even if you live to be a hundred and ten – "as a little child you cannot enter the Kingdom of Heaven." Go back to school with Jesus as your form master. Recognise that this life is a childhood preparing for the adult world of heaven: and yet paradoxically you don't have to wait until you die. The lesson involves a radical reversal of the values of this world, will involve facing, living with, accepting and redeeming the dark side of your life, breaking through to joy even in physical suffering, loneliness and bereavement: knowing that the lesson involves knowing and unknowing – and as our eyes are opened, acknowledging some other ordinary men and women, who for all their faults and failures have triumphed in love, and are fellow citizens in the Kingdom of Heaven on earth, and in Heaven. Like Jean Vanier, Sheila Cassidy – and, why not, Matt Busby and

Brian Redhead as well.

Look around – you may hear someone saying, "so *you're* here, how lovely", or have your own mouth opened to say to the last person you ever thought of, "Fancy meeting you! – I'm so glad."

The Holocaust

The wisdom of this world is folly in God's sight.   *1 Cor 3:19*

Preached on the Anniversary of the Holocaust
February 1995

T HERE are three images of human pain which have, in the past weeks, had the power to overwhelm all others, even the most personal disasters which affect us all from time to time.

In a sense all those events are but the same thing writ large – very large indeed, beyond our power to imagine, even though television has the ability to describe them visually – but not the pain, not the smell, not the *feel* of it; not the internal desolation.

Firstly there was, there is, the continuing conflict in Bosnia, slowed down for a while by the snow and the bitter cold which seems to have little effect in Chechenya where old men and women fled from cellar to cellar in a city systematically smashed to rubble by Russian tanks and troops.

Then there is the horror story of the earthquake in Japan, the full extent of which is still coming to light; followed by the flooding in Europe – both "natural" disasters leading to more homelessness.

And hovering over it all, the fiftieth anniversary of the Holocaust. One thing which will live with me for ever is the cold horror of truth as I heard a survivor from the gas chambers describe how he escaped while millions were murdered.

He was saved quite simply because he was a barber, forced to cut off the hair of women and girls paraded naked

36

before him just before their barbaric deaths. He is now an elderly man in, I suppose, his early seventies, still cutting hair, who with dignity tried to contain his grief, but broke down in front of the camera as he told how the young man next to him was obliged to cut off the hair of his mother and sister, suddenly in front of him there in the gas chamber, his farewell before he saw them go to die.

For us as for them it must raise the old cry, "Behold and see if there be any sorrow like unto my sorrow".

It raises as well the old, impossible question, the possibly terrifying and for many the seemingly unanswerable question of faith in God, which lies at the heart of this paradoxical text, "The wisdom of this world is folly in God's sight". Or as it is says elsewhere in this same Epistle, "the folly of God is wiser than the wisdom of men, and the divine weakness stronger than man's strength".

We know this very well on a personal level when faith is challenged. The sudden discovery of terminal disease already far gone, the painful search for words of comfort, for explanations, encouragement, and sometimes the failure to find them. The desertion or betrayal of someone you love deeply, the overwhelming finality of death when it strikes our immediate circle of friends or relatives, the isolation of bereavement. All those are the material of our mortality, inescapable elements in our human condition. And you say, "Why God, why?"

The question is not new. The most penetrating analysis of it is to be found in the Book of Job. The trouble is that the answers it proposes can ring in our ears as a little hollow. In the beginning it is, after all, God who lets the wicked Angel, Satan, free to torment the godly man Job with the deaths of his children, the decimation of his flocks, and to cover him with boils. This surely is an unbelievable God. No more believable than the end of the story in which he comes up with a supernatural "lottery" of a vast family, flocks and luxurious old age!

We say, "It is He that hath made us and not we ourselves,

we are his people", or "Herein is God, not that we loved Him but that He first loved us". So what about the earthquakes and the floods? Are we such fools as to suppose the Church is committed to finding an answer?

Where our personal pains are concerned there are human answers to the human condition, and our chief hope lies in the acknowledgement within ourselves of a God of love who in Jesus has accepted and lived through just the same pain, isolation, desolation. For faith in God at the time depends on the acceptance that the numbness will wear off, the actual pain diminish, the isolation become bearable, and new creative life creep on us in something like a new birth that is nothing less than a rediscovery of God. God beyond the grave. Not forgetting what is past – but a past enhanced by a grief accepted, observed and recreated for others as well as ourselves.

But the impact of deliberate cruelty on such a vast scale as the annihilation of six million Jews is for a conscious Christian not just a sociological question but a profoundly religious one. *They* were the first to say, "We are his people and the sheep of his pasture". They were the "chosen people". For several complex reasons Jews are still widely mistrusted, not least superficially because of their apparent domination of the financial world. But the crucial question, so graphically presented to me yet again by those piles of skeleton bodies, the rail track on a bleak landscape which led to the huts, the chambers, the furnaces, the casual brutality or the S.S., all this human folly is apparently answered by one man, and him a Jew, all contained in this one Jewish life and death. A death like His which has all the same physical torture, prolonged pain, an insensitive, cruel disregard of dignity, even of humanity itself.

The foolishness of God lies in the incomprehensible fact that He could call into being a world which functions in such a way – as the home for men and women who could develop a race which from among them could produce Bach and Beethoven – and then from among the millions condemned to death save the musicians who as captives would play their music as the stream of man's fellow Jews were murdered. As they were forced to. Sheer madness. The madness of man.

The folly of God is that He died with each one of them. He a fellow Jew. The pity, the eternal pity for all the Jewish people, is that they did not believe it, and still don't. And for us the astonishing reality which we can only dimly comprehend, is that for us who, for all our wisdom as Christians, have so far to go in understanding, the challenge is to accept that we too are sufficient fools as to believe that we are one with the Jews in claiming the same Father God who called us all into becoming Christians; and one with this fallen humanity for all of whom He died – Christians and Jews, believer and unbeliever; and whose final cry – a cry of the same human pain as we all share – is, "Father forgive them they don't know what they are doing".

The ultimate folly of God is that He *does* forgive. The ultimate folly of man is to fail to recognise that this is indeed, for us *all*, the only - Final Solution.

The Pity of God

THE ANNIVERSARY
OF THE END OF THE WAR

Love one another, just as I have loved you.
John 15:12

AS a boy I remember an old man – well he must have been at least fifty – telling me about how he had fought in the Boer War: the first war of this century in which we were involved as a nation; the first war in which trenches were used.

The war in Europe, the First Great War, exploited trenches to a devastating effect, and millions were trapped in them, suffocated in mud, or poison gas, bayoneted and bombed: in a war the scars of which remain to this day. That was the war to end wars – the old man had fought in that as well, though as is always the case, it was a young man's war. I grew up in the shadow of it, as a defeated Germany rearmed to terrifying totalitarian power. There was, of course, the League of Nations, which many believed would preserve Peace. Twenty years after the Armistice, Neville Chamberlain returned from Hitler in Munich, to say, "Out of the nettle of danger, I have plucked the flower of Peace." But they still dug trenches in Hyde Park and I joined the Territorial Army – a regiment in south London.

So I went along with the boy who lived next door, and all the local lads, who for the most part used the same local pubs and played in the same teams, had in many cases been to the same schools. We trained together and, when the war began, moved off. I missed going to France, missed the offensives – and the retreat to Dunkirk when a great many of them were killed. And I was left with a sense of

40

guilt that has never entirely left me – that I was not with them. We had all stood, in the words of Frances Cornford:

Dreaming on the verge of strife,
Magnificently unprepared, for the long littleness of life.

I find it hard to forgive a world which repeatedly misuses power and destroys so many millions of young men and women – German, Russian and Japanese as well – in such wasteful defiance of God in Creation. So in common with everyone I focus at first on personal loss. But the commemorations of this weekend conclude a series of corporate recollections: largely of the endless sophistication of destruction, as war was no longer left to the armies, but became the total involvement of all humanity – which in a sense has been always the case. In the Boer War dispatches were sent from the front taking weeks. Modern technology has enabled us to relive the terrifying horror of the Holocaust, the final solution for six million Jews, of the Gulag Archipelago and the ruthless tyranny of Stalin, of the destruction of Coventry and London in flames – and the relentless hordes of British and American bombers, who in wave after wave reduced Dresden and all its people to a flaming furnace; of the wasteland of Hiroshima; and this weekend, the accounts of prisoners at the hands of the Japanese soldiers, which both horrify in the telling, and astound at the endurance of those who remain.

We naturally give thanks that we too remain to tell – and acknowledge that for fifty years there has been no war on this scale. A generation of young men have grown up without war. But there *have* been wars since 1945 – some of which have involved our own forces – and there is Bosnia on our doorstep.

How do we sort this out with God?

Individually it will always be a personal matter. We bring to God our own needs. So far as forgiveness is concerned there are always the words of Jesus who taught us

41

to pray, "forgive us our sins as we forgive those who sin against us". We might find it hard to forgive a society which for whatever reason finds war the only solution to its needs, the politicians who make the decision, or the generals who carry them out, and easier perhaps to forgive the young Germans, Russians or Japanese, who only carried out orders. But here we already embark on after-dinner conversation in speculation. So if what you are left with as a prayer is, "Father forgive me for not being able to forgive," well, it is clumsy, but as honest as can be managed, and He knows what you mean. It applies as much to many other aspects and times of life.

Jesus also said, "Father forgive them, they do not know what they are doing". And that applies to us as well. In the Gospel, He tells us to love one another, and that love crosses all boundaries and barriers or is intended to. Love your enemy, he says, bless those who persecute you. Well at the time he said "Father forgive", he was exposed to just the sort of brutality of which we have heard and seen so much in the films and commentaries.

It is the memory of that event which is the heart of this celebration of Holy Communion. We deliberately recall it. But the declaration of faith which follows has a note of triumph. "Christ has died." "He died that we might be forgiven", we sing, but add, "Christ is risen", and "Christ will come again".

In all our recollections of the past, and honouring of the dead, as we should, Christ comes again, to point the way to Peace, to a risen life in this world and a personal victory we can share with him in this life. That is what love means – the victory of forgiveness creating a new life of love – in this world.

In one of the greatest of war poems, Wilfred Owen speaks of

> the pity of war,
> the pity war distils.

42

The presence of Jesus in the world is the ultimate expression of the pity of God for the whole human race. Because He alone knows the full power of human sin, He who never sinned – He alone knows the full power of forgiveness – and in his pity for us He gave his life.

Let William Blake, who struggled as much as anyone with this – trying to reconcile the overwhelming glory of God with the enormity of man's misuse of his creation – say a last word for us, of gratitude for all the men and women who fought for Peace, as we also try in honesty to find a way of living with our own loyalty in love to God and mankind.

> To Mercy, Pity, Peace and Love
> All pray in their distress
> And to these virtues of delight
> Return their thankfulness.
>
> For Mercy, Pity, Peace and Love
> Is God our Father dear
> And Mercy, Pity, Peace and Love
> Is Man, his child and care.
>
> For Mercy has a human heart
> Pity a human face
> And Love the human form Divine
> And Peace the human dress.
>
> Then every man of every clime
> That prays in his distress
> Prays to the human form divine
> Love, Mercy, Pity, Peace.

The Voice of Strangers

They will run away from him: because they
do not recognize the voice of strangers.

John 10:5

I RECENTLY became involved in one of those slightly
embarrassing social incidents which are a familiar part
of life – at any rate of mine. It was after the Bar Mitzvah of
the son of a friend – for me a totally new and moving experience with some echoes of my own confirmation over sixty
years ago. At the luncheon which followed I was put to sit
next to a complete stranger who, I discovered, was a distinguished sociologist, and a slightly formidable lady. Well
someone has to start the conversation so I said, "I don't
think we've met before but somehow I think I know you".
She replied rather firmly that we certainly had *not* met.
Then her face brightened a little and she said, "But I expect
you saw me on television last night". I had to confess that
I hardly ever watch television, though I do listen quite
often to the radio, so perhaps it was her voice I recalled.
Her face became a little more fixed, and I never quite recovered the lost ground. After all, I hadn't read her books
either!

But her voice was distinctive, and indeed Radio Four can
make one vividly aware of the variety and particularity of
the human voice. You don't need the face, just listen! The
conceit, the fraud, the fear, the downright lies behind the
truth or even the truth behind the all too apparent lies, the
bitter and the bold, the lovely and the loveless, the power
of simple words in a valid voice. At present all those voices
in Los Angeles, complaining, explaining, betraying a terrifying anger and fear, faced with political, racial, and social
problems of a complexity that has put the race for the

44

Presidency into a new perspective. Of course we have as many problems here, some of them similar, and having survived the torrents of words, and the all too shrill voices of the general election, there is still a hangover as Brian Gould and John Smith slog it out.

Auden suggests:

> A sentence uttered makes a world appear
> Where all things happen as they say they do
> We doubt the speaker, not the tongue we hear
> Words have no words for words that are not true

So much for the voices of strangers. No wonder there is, in the world, a profound distrust in almost every part of public life. But what of the familiar voice, the voice we know?

At first glance the parable about the Good Shepherd, which clearly has a lengthy, important and prominent place in the teaching of Jesus, could seem a bit remote from our world, unless perhaps you are a farmer, in which case you might still feel obliged to listen to the voice of a Minister defending British lambs from the French.

Jesus is suggesting an intimacy and commitment in love between shepherd and sheep which goes far beyond the merely simple or sentimental to a care which is absolute to the point, if necessary, of sacrifice and death. "I lay down my life for the sheep." And this applies not only to Him, but to all those men and women who in every generation share his ministry of care for the people of God – bishops, priests and deacons.

Well, the sheep are not as silly as they look, they can hear and know a voice they trust. It so happens that the Archdeacon (who is I suppose also a sort of arch shepherd) has a wife who is an absolute authority on, of all things, the voices of animals and sheep in particular! She has researched with sheep all over the world, but in particular with one flock of which she monitored every single voice, each of them individual and distinctive. Not only do they know the voice of the shepherd, but the lambs all know the voice of their mothers, and will go to no other. So it is not so far fetched.

The allegory of the Shepherd and the sheep has a very significant place in the Bible which is, for Christians, not only the Word of God but the Voice of God. It is not for nothing that some Christians, and Christian ministers in particular repeat every day of their lives: "Today if you will hear his voice harden not your hearts." "We are his people and the sheep of his pasture."

The Bible story has its origin in the beginning with a man called by God, responding to the Voice, the spiritual father of the human race (and incidentally of Jews, Moslems, Christians alike) Abraham, who was prepared to show his fidelity to the Voice by sacrificing his son. And before we dismiss that as primitive, even savage, it is necessary to remember that it has strong echoes in this service with its message of sacrifice.

It is picked up more specifically in the dramatic, even romantic, and true history of David, the shepherd king, the poet and singer, whose voice is heard in the psalms, whose royalty gives validity to his descendant the baby King born in a stable at Bethlehem, of David's line, as we his family sing at Christmas. Jesus is the supreme Shepherd King who said, "I am the good Shepherd", ready if necessary to die for my sheep. Who knows each one of us personally, individually, with our individual voice. It is a situation that is never without conflict. There are false shepherds. So far as the Jews, the old Israel, were concerned, they were only too ready to be seduced by the voice of strangers.

But this is the whole history of mankind, not merely of Israel. After all, it was the persuasive voice of Satan that got us off to a wrong start in the Garden of Eden. It is no less persuasive today whether you live in a garden suburb or among the lavish lawns of your favourite college. Never were words and voices more persuasive or cynically or misleadingly used than under such ideal or idealistic conditions. So from King David to Jesus, the voices listened to least and frequently silenced, were the voices that denounced the false shepherds, strangers to the truth: and so far as Jesus was concerned, the only possible end for so much truth was death. What Abraham was restrained from offering to God in those dark distant beginnings – his only son – was offered by Jesus himself to God the Father, the sacrifice which we commemorate in this service of Holy Communion, a service in which we hear the words of John the Baptist – "Lamb of God who takes away the sin of the world have mercy on us".

All this was brought home to me at the Bar Mitzvah. I was deeply impressed, indeed moved by it. The reverence paid to the Scrolls of the Law as it was processed through the synagogue, the readings, the word of God also familiar to us, reminders of Moses, of David, of Amos, the Psalms, and the prayers – prayers of Christians as well as of Jews.

And then suddenly a strange emptiness. I had been brought to a new awareness of my Jewish origins in faith, as I am every day when I say Morning and Evening Prayer – which indeed contain more Old Testament than New. Yet it is there in the New Testament I find myself – I hear a Voice, a Personal Voice. That service reminded me of my own Confirmation, at just the same age – in a church in London in 1929. I preached there last Sunday, looking down on the very spot, remembering it as if it were yesterday. What was so different from the Bar Mitzvah? That church laid the foundation of my faith, I can't remember the words – I am deeply conscious of the Voice. I discovered there without knowing it, the valid questions which have answers beyond words. About holiness and goodness, which has nothing at all to do with being goody goody. About mystery, and beauty, and a sense of the transcendent more real than any reality. About prayer having little to do with words, but in which heart speaks to heart. That to be in Love is to be in a condition of trust and surrender which has more than a merely personal identity yet invests persons with a freedom that almost defies imagination, that truth is not a mere arrangement of words and that above all things an authentic voice can finally only be heard by the heart and not the head alone.

Above all this, and it makes all the difference, to discover that at the centre of the Gospel is not just a message but a man – a man whose distinctive voice has all the familiarity of a friend or lover, who shares my vulnerability, my fear, who shared my life as man, that I might share his life in God, and through whose eyes I can see the world as God sees it; and whose voice leads me to where I can recognise the path of truth, and encourages me to take it; who does not always make my life comfortable, but makes it possible, possible to live with myself, live with others, to have life as he says, which is abundant life, not just more of it. That makes it possible for me to say with integrity, "The Lord is my Shepherd – and though I walk through the valley of the shadow of death I will fear no evil" – for with Him I might even distinguish the voice of truth from the voice of strangers.

On Old Age

My eyes have seen thy salvation.

Luke 2:30

LORD, the Roman Hyacinths are
    blooming in bowls, and
The winter sun creeps by the snow hills
The stubborn season has made stand
My life is light waiting for the death wind.

Eliot has sympathy for Simeon, not least because he is old – has waited so long. But then Eliot is concerned elsewhere with old age:

I grow old I grow old
I shall wear the bottoms of my trousers rolled.

Indeed I do. But more pointedly and almost another reference to the old man in the Temple holding Jesus in his arms he says elsewhere:

What was to be the value of the long
    looked forward to,
Long hoped for calm, the autumnal serenity
And the wisdom of Age.

I was given last week by a generous friend a bowl of hyacinths, which have just bloomed in time for this most eloquent of ancient traditions in our Church, Candlemas, a celebration of age – nicely contrived by the Gospel writers to balance Adam and Eve. Old Simeon with Old Anna, and even perhaps a hint of the baby's grandmother too, the mother of Mary, St Anne.

Is it my imagination, or does it not seem that so much of the story of Jesus in the Gospel is reflected in the lives of *young* men and women. After all Jesus himself died at the

49

age of only thirty-three – by then it was all over. His first fishermen friends and disciples left their father's business to follow him. The narrative has all the drive and urgency of new discoveries being made by those who early in life are charting the future.

How true it seemed of our own age – at least until recently. The ball was at the feet of the young and enterprising, bright eyes, sharply dressed, living at ease off large mortgages – whether in the stockbroker belts of the home counties or the council estates of enterprise zones in the industrial north. All based on predictions of expansion, financial growth, private ownership. Then came the recession.

Something else was also happening to upset the calculations. People are living longer, their life expectancy has changed. The end no longer is fixed at three score years and ten. Old age has been overcome by Third Age. Redundancies and retirement at fifty-five or sixty are forcing people to face the prospect of twenty years or more lying ahead of them. To some a daunting even terrifying prospect, to others, time to be frenetically filled, to yet others a real gift of time to be planned, enjoyed, a time for new life, a time of freedom filled with expectation.

How sad that some seem only to "stand waiting for the death wind", while for others "autumnal serenity and the wisdom of old age".

How much does this matter to those who are still young in years – I know that many of the old are, or intend to be, young in heart. Well possibly the most significant miscalculation where the setting up of the Welfare State was concerned was a failure to recognise the strain which a much older population would place on the Health Service and the Social Services in general, particularly when coupled with the advances in medical practice which have enabled us to keep going so much longer. Old age, or older age is, to that extent, at their expense. Keeping people alive is very costly. Is it worth it? Men and women in the Bible who lived to a conspicuously old age are mentioned for that very reason – with their ages sometimes exaggerated a little to make the point. Anna was 84. For one reason or another people by our standards then died young; as is still the case for the Third World, indeed probably for the majority of people in the world.

In our world an increasing number of the elderly end their days in a "Home" of one kind or another, shut away, no doubt under conditions sometimes of monumental middle class respectability, but not infrequently in something like a slightly crowded ghetto where every idiosyncrasy is emphasised, every shortcoming or weakness, every oddity is carefully or cruelly monitored by the rest, and the pervading sense of monotony is ill concealed by trivial pursuits. Yes, I know it's not always like that. By contrast, with all the deprivations of the undeveloped countries, the treasure they retain is the living presence of the elderly among them as part of their lives.

I realise that this is beginning to sound like a plug for Help the Aged or Age Concern. Well, I certainly have a concern – but the help might be better recognised the other way round. To what end has God given us this old age? How awful if retirement feels like rejection – filling in time, "waiting for my turn to go".

There is a spirituality of old age which is a powerful resource for the whole Christian community, and beyond those boundaries to the whole world. There is indeed something to be said for the long hoped for calm, the autumnal serenity and the wisdom of old age, but those sentiments are almost sentimental, and old age has its own toughness, is bigger than that.

What Simeon says is, "My eyes have seen thy salvation, which thou hast prepared before the face of all people". He is not alone, traditionally it was the old St John who was left waiting by Jesus, who long after the heady days in Galilee of his first discipleship wrote, "that which our eyes have seen, that which our hands have handled of the word of life declare we unto you."

The ceremony of Candlemas links us with Easter Eve, when a candle lit by new fire is carried into the middle of the congregation while we proclaim, "The light of Christ. Thanks be to God." Today we thank God for the acknowledgement of that light not just by the chosen people of God – but a light for all mankind. It is that light which shows up the world for what it really is, and that light is not a flickering candle but a living being – the Lord Jesus Christ.

Perhaps old age has been given to us because in our increasingly complex world, where human values are so cruelly distorted, we need those who with greater perspective in time, and a life of prayer and action tested by the years, can hold up Jesus and say: "My eyes have seen thy salvation", and, far from living on the margin of our spiritual life, can reveal that the Third Age is the age of prayer, of new discovery, the age of the Spirit, a resource for the whole Body of Christ helping them to say also: "My eyes have seen", and handing over to others a living Lord – the Light of Christ.

Praying for Unity

That they all may be one – that the world may believe.   *John 17:21*

I RETURNED on Friday from a holiday in time to share in the Diocesan Pilgrimage to Walsingham. Walsingham has been a place of prayer for centuries and each year over 100,000 travel from all over England to pray in their own way – interceding for the world, the Church, and their own personal needs and those for whom they are concerned.

The question of prayer on holiday is an interesting one. In theory we are relaxed, away from it all – so there's lots more time to pray in and indeed some people spend their holidays in places like Walsingham. On the other hand it is holiday – so why not a holiday from prayer? Have a rest, and, if it doesn't seem too irreverent, give God a rest too from all our searchings and confusions. I suppose it depends on what sort of holiday you have. Mine included a great deal of time by myself – no phone, no letters, and every morning after breakfast a long leisurely read of the daily paper with an extra cup of coffee to keep it company. In the evening a little selective television. As a result the contemplation of God, and the place of prayer has a way of not so much intruding, as just being there, a reminder that even if God rested on his seventh day and hallowed it – our divisions between work and play are artificial. Indeed *some* people work so hard at their holidays they find it a relief to get back – and to a lot of us eating can just be boring.

All of which came to mind one day last week as I contemplated the preparation of a sermon on prayer – and read my favourite newspaper.

Because of the Olympic Games I turned first to the back page – and was captivated by a picture I shall long remember. Kriss Akabusi is a brilliant young athlete who had won a gold medal in the 400 metres hurdles. Not only that, but to his own amazement he also set a new United Kingdom record. It was an occasion for jubilation. Akabusi is a great favourite, charming, lively, friendly, generous. And there, quite spontaneously and without thinking what he was doing, overwhelmed by what had happened, he fell on his knees, there in the Stadium at Split, and thanked God. No, he is not a Moslem but recognised as a Christian, who conducts a daily prayer meeting with a few fellow athletes. There are doubtless those who pray for victory in Kuwait – why not give thanks for a victory in Split? It was notable that nobody mocked – everyone admired. So much for the back page.

The *front* page was a different matter altogether. An account of perhaps the most painful and heart searching journalistic interview in recent history. Brian Keenan, clearly a man of deep sensitivity, choosing exact and expressive words with pain and many pauses – taking us with him into the close confines of captivity. I found it hard to read the words again. The report said:

> Mr Keenan said he had never been religious but added "One can't keep the mind alive by talking to itself. You have to grasp out at something else, which gives you a sense of your own validity. If you're asking me, Did I pray, *Yes*; if you're asking me if I am religious, No."

I understand that for a long time – years – the only book allowed the hostages was the Koran - in much the same way as we might give Moslems in this country a Gideon's Bible. Was it in the Koran that Brian Keenan grasped at something which gave him a sense of his own validity?

It is a question which has some pertinence today, because the particular prayer to which I have been invited to direct you is prayer for unity. Prayer for the unity, that is, of the Christian Church. For a long time there has been established a group of churches united in their intention to work

54

and pray for the Unity of Christendom – the World Council of Churches, and, in this country, the British Council of Churches. There were some who felt unable to join that body, notably some strict Baptists and the whole Roman Catholic Church. The doctrinal and religious reasons that created the barrier, at any rate so far as the Roman Catholics are concerned, have been overcome and a new organisation is being launched. *Churches Together in England,* the Council of Churches for Britain and Ireland.

On any showing this is a striking and significant event. Those with long memories will remember the entrenched and frequently bitter antagonism, suspicion and superstitious fear on both sides – Protestant and Catholic – which once seemed insurmountable. Indeed it would be false to suggest that this is not still the case in some quarters, notably in Ireland. But there is hope in this new initiative. You can't keep a Church, Anglican, Methodist, United Reformed, Catholic, alive by talking to itself – you have to grasp out at something else. In the context of our divided Christendom, such a fearful scandal to the world, and part of the religion Brian Keenan and so many others reject, prayer for unity can spring from an innate sense of the death to self which is ours when we go it alone. That sounds desperate – but then the Church of England, to speak for ourselves, is trapped to its own religious diminishment and captivity.

I also saw last week the television repeat of the *Barchester Chronicles.* Trollope is so timeless.

The incentive which leads us to pray for unity carries with it more than desperation. The ultimate and glorious incentive comes from Christ himself. To grasp at God is to be given a glimpse of my own validity – indeed, but it is in Christ that validity is made known to me in a reality, which is both his and mine.

What lay behind the prayer of Jesus for unity was not just the unity of his immediate followers, from which

55

sprang our divided Church, but the unity of all those to whom he had ministered.

I can never forget the impact made on me by the great mosque in Jerusalem, the heart of Christianity, but the heart also for Jews and Moslems. That great golden dome stands over the Rock – the rock on which Abraham was prepared to offer Isaac, his only son to God – Abraham the father we all have in common, Christians, Moslems, Jews.

While we talk about the unity of Christians, Moslems are preparing to offer their sons, Christians are preparing to offer their sons – for what? for *oil*. Would we truly prepare to offer as much to God – for Himself?

I am profoundly glad that this new initiative towards the unity of Christians in Britain has been given to us – and I want to call on you, as all the congregations in this country are being called, to share in pledging ourselves to that end. The world outside the Church offers us a great challenge. The upsurge of Islam can be seen as a threat, a call to a holy war, but surely it should be seen as God calling us to a renewed humanity. For us that means a renewed divinity, a revitalising of our part in the life of Jesus, the Son already offered.

As we respond to him, so let us respond to his prayer – that they all may be one, that the world may believe – and they *will* believe, if the Christ we offer in our lives is not the fractured Christ of our divisions, but the whole, the complete Christ of our common life in Him – a Christ in which the exuberant born-again Akabusi, and the heart-searching Brian Keenan can recognise and love each other – and all of us as well.

The First Friars in Cambridge
THE JOHN MERE SERMON

---

1 Cor. 15:54,55

---

*John Mere is buried in St Bene't's churchyard. He endowed a
sermon to be preached annually in St Bene't's Church before
the Vice Chancellor and the University*

SOME time in the year 1235 the first Franciscan friars
appeared in Cambridge town. Barefoot, ragged,
paupers, begging for food and accommodation. It was only
a few years after a considerably larger group of scholars
had arrived here and helped in the foundation of the
University. Unknowingly the foundations were also laid of
an association between them which flourished for nearly
three hundred years and enriched them both.

The friars were first offered accommodation in a
dwelling known as the House of Benjamin the Jew,
probably situated close to the present Guildhall. Formerly
a synagogue it was by this time used, in part, as a jail. The
friars were given the other half and remained there for
forty years in increasing discomfort as their numbers grew
considerably.

The townsfolk then helped them to build a new Friary on
the site of what is now Sidney Sussex College, where they
remained until the final dissolution of the monasteries in
1538 when it passed into the hands of Trinity College and
was pulled down, the building becoming a quarry for the
construction of the Chapel and Great Court – with its foun-
tain fed by the conduit once built by the friars themselves.

John Mere, who died in 1558, would have known the

57

remaining friars who were dispersed at that time; had possibly gathered with other citizens in the big Franciscan church, built for preaching to great crowds – and frequently used by the University for their public occasions. He might also have hoped to be buried there. The Friary was a favourite place for funerals, and a considerable part of the friars' income came from the saying of masses for the departed. A contemporary of his, perhaps a fellow parishioner, one Nicholas Symond, desired in 1533 that his funeral should be held here in St Benedict's Church after which three friars were to carry his body to the Church of the Grey Friars for burial.

If John Mere had hoped to emulate him, the hope was frustrated by Henry VIII. Although by the time of his death there was a new Prayer Book – the ASB of the sixteenth century, though considerably more radical in its innovations and more distinguished in its language – it was not widely in use, and John Mere probably had read over him the old funeral rite. But he was buried in the churchyard here, and the money that might have gone to masses for the repose of his soul went to sermons for the edification of others. The friars to carry his coffin had all gone.

However, for the past fifty years it has once again been possible to muster three or four friars for that purpose in Cambridge - indeed for most of that time there have been friars as priests of this parish, so on this admittedly tenuous connection between his day and ours I would like to turn my thoughts and earn my pence by considering the admonition in his bequest concerning death and our preparation for it – not least because it was a concern of St Francis, the father of the first friars in Cambridge, who was preparing for his own death which occurred in 1226 only a year after they arrived, and of the latter day Anglican friars who in some sense have entered into their inheritance.

Francis lived for only forty-four years. About half way through that life he abandoned a home of modest luxury and a carefree life and became a wandering barefoot beggar in rags. Starting with nothing but the derision of his friends and the enmity of his father, he attracted a following of thousands. At a meeting of his brothers in Assisi three years before he died, there were over 5000 present – and then from there dispersing to reach out all over Europe and beyond. Though many of his followers were simple, others were scholars who within a generation were making a significant mark in the universities, not least in Cambridge.

What *was* his attraction? He had a sort of passion for poverty, calling Poverty his Bride – a passion for the poor, the deprived, the sick, the lepers of all kinds; he had a passion for solitude, for listening to God – this above all things. He had too a passion – and the word is not a misplaced exaggeration – for people. Yet he was no crank, no thirteenth century hippy or drop-out – and neither were the men and women drawn to him. I suspect people sometimes feared him as much as they loved him – I do myself, and I've known him, as it were, for half a century. But who would not stand in awe of such absolute, such completely natural and open love, such uncomplicated humanity? So what is it and how did it affect his approach to death? His attitude to death only makes sense as we appreciate his attitude to life; and his attitude to life sprang from his total surrender to God.

His conversion was the result of a series of blinding flashes of, for him, inescapable insight, each of which led him to a deeper knowledge of God and, as a consequence, knowledge of himself. How do you respond if you deliberately ask God what you should do with your life – and God says "Build a church"? For him there was no question – go and build it. It was only the beginning and in fact he didn't quite get the answer right. But he was a quick learner. What do you do if you suddenly see a leper, a mass of oozing sores as if for the first time, and the only answer appears to be – kiss him, hug him, heal him. You learn much more from doing that. And if your father takes you to court and accuses you of stealing from him – only one thing seems right, you take off every stitch of clothing and give it back to him. No wonder at first they thought he was mad.

But he left his father, his home, his friends, everything and everyone, and lived for nearly three years alone in caves and abandoned churches, begging for food, and listening to God, learning how to see the world through the eyes of God, recognising the familiar sights in a startling new way as if for the first time. And not only seeing them, but relating to them with an intimacy, a reality and completeness that has rarely been achieved before or since. Chesterton says of him that he was a man who did not want to see the wood for the trees, he wanted to see each tree as a separate, almost a sacred thing. And what was true for trees was true for every single person he met – seeing them as separate, as sacred, seeing them as God sees them, and all of us, sharing the life of God as He in Jesus Christ shared our humanity. So Jesus was central to his thinking, his whole being. In the long silences and solitudes of prayer he grew in the awareness and reality of God's participation in our lives, each one of us, and as a direct and complete consequence our participation in His.

The reality of that for St Francis was so intense, his identification with Jesus so real that towards the end of his life, while alone in prayer, the visible marks of the life and death of Christ appeared in his hands, feet and side. This is, we know, a phenomenon that has occurred in the life of other mystics, both men and women, and could be explained on psychological grounds. In the life of Francis it seems, to those who come to know him well enough, entirely congruous with the rest of his life.

His discovery – and it is an open secret – was that the best preparation for death was an overwhelming acceptance of life. John Mere asked that the preacher should exhort his congregation to the daily preparation for death and not to fear it. Francis prepared not only every day but in a true sense every moment of every day. Like Paul he could say "I die daily" and that he always "carried around in his own body the dying of the Lord Jesu".

His life lived out the paradox with which we are all faced. Abandoning all personal possessions of any kind he yet inherited the world, in every particular, calling all Creation his brother and sister. Abandoning the usual responsibilities of parents and family, he undertook without hesitation the responsibility of seeing all people as his brothers and sisters, finding freedom in love most particularly for the sick, the poor, the lonely and rejected. So death was no stranger to be feared, or ignored, or shut away. Alive today he would be as instantly among the victims of AIDS, as he ministered to lepers: or camping among the Kurds as readily as he went to the Crusaders to campaign for peace.

In the last years of his life, sick himself and almost blind, in intense pain from the primitive surgery of his time, he not only retained the exuberant joy, the laughter and song which had characterised his life but found new outlets for it. Not least in the great poem we know as *The Canticle of the Sun*, in which he catalogues the many ways he had come to know God in his creation. It begins:

> Praise be my Lord God by all his creatures, and especially our brother the Sun who brings us the day and brings us the light. Fair is he and shines with a very great splendour. O Lord he signifies to us Thee.

He then goes on to extol the moon, stars, the earth, summer and winter, flowers and grass. When it comes to man he recognises our need to be free from sin if we are to really enter into possession of the world. Sin, after all, is just the diminishing of our whole lives by various forms, and by various degrees, of selfishness. So he says, "Praise be my Lord by those who pardon one another for his love's sake." If you can forgive, and let yourself be forgiven, you can properly possess the world, truly embrace life. But he concludes, "Praise be my Lord for our Sister the death of the body, from which no man escapes. Woe to him who dies in sin." To be unforgiving, to be unforgiven – that we might fear, for it traps us in this world to such a degree that we not only fail to enter the freedom of truly living this life, but also find ourselves prevented from enjoying the freedom of death which liberates us into the eternal, the resurrection life.

Francis on his own deathbed rather shocked those who stood by. Already recognised as a saint it seemed improper that he should be so happy about dying, sharing the experience with his Brothers, singing his canticle exuberantly, and crying out "Welcome Sister Death", a sister who was in no sense a stranger but rather a companion who had always been with him – one of the family.

The friars who arrived here, begging for their food, and living together in one room, next to all the scoundrels in Cambridge, were in time replaced by brothers of outstanding ability and learning who made a major contribution to the foundation of the faculty of theology. Yet the example of the life of Francis in its simplicity and directness has persisted over all the centuries. In a world where death from violence of all kinds or death from natural disaster is so vividly communicated to us by the mass media it seems as if only the most shocking of personal events has power to penetrate our defences and remind us that death, sudden or delayed, is the one certainty from which we all have no escape. The capsizing of a ferry boat we all might have used, the crushing to death at a football match we all might have attended, the sudden death of a contemporary, a colleague – the sudden shock of recognising "He was my age" with the unspoken "it might have been me" that is true, at any age.

Francis encourages us to live in such a way as makes that moment even welcome. In this season of Easter our ears still hear the familiar hymn which echoes a reality which is as true for Francis and us as I pray it was for John

Mere. "Jesus lives, henceforth is death but the gate of life immortal."

He could not in his day have paid the friars for a Mass; but this morning in this Church we prayed for him at the Eucharist, and I accept with gratitude his pence for the Sermon, and repeat:

> Rest eternal grant unto him, O Lord
> And let light perpetual shine upon him.
> May he rest in Peace. Amen.

Monks and Nuns

A VOCATION

We are the impostors who speak the truth,
the unknown men whom all men know;
dying we still live on; disciplined by
suffering, we are not done to death; in our
sorrows we have always cause for joy;
poor ourselves, we bring wealth to many;
penniless, we own the world.   *2 Cor 6:8-10*

THE immediate neighbours of St Bene't's Church include the delightful sixteenth century building called Friars' House. It might be thought that it is related to the presence of Franciscans in St Bene't's. Not so. There was indeed a time when there were friars living in Bene't Street – but they were Augustinian and the monastery stretched down to Barclays Bank. It is even thought that the 16th century pub across the road, aptly named "The Bath", is on the site of their old Bath House.

In fact the Franciscans in those days lived on the site of what is now Sidney Sussex College, and their Friary included a very big chapel and extensive grounds. These, divided by a lane, ran alongside the grounds of a convent which eventually became Jesus College.

This church of St Benedict was possibly related in some way with the great Abbey at Ely a few miles away. At the beginning of the sixteenth century, monks and nuns of all kinds were everywhere and for ordinary people went without question as part of daily life, even if some grumbled. Some of the grumbles were justified. The convent in Jesus Lane only had a handful of nuns. Some monks seemed morally lax, and some monasteries were very rich and powerful. But not all, and though there may have been room for reform there were those who maintained monastic discipline and prayer.

The reforms, and finally the destruction came quickly at the hand of Henry VIII, partly to assert his supremacy and certainly because they were rich and he needed money. In 1536 an act was passed to close the smaller monasteries and three years later another to dissolve all the major ones – like Ely – and by 1540 it was all over, ruthlessly, violently, thoroughly. There were no more monks and nuns. At Ely the last Prior of the Abbey became the first Dean of the Cathedral and was immediately faced with a series of difficulties, not least the question of how to continue the prayers – which is what the monasteries were all about.

When men become monks – and this applies in different ways to friars, nuns, sisters, all who generally live as part of a religious community – they enter a monastery as they say "to seek God", the whole structure of their life in the monastery has that end. It is not for themselves alone – even though they know in their hearts that it is the only way in which they might be saved. Indeed it is one reason why they come to recognise the truth for them, when he says that he came to call not the righteous but sinners. Religious are not in any way chosen by God because they are already holy – indeed they are frequently rather confused or inadequate people who have come to realise, sometimes to their dismay or astonishment, that while God chooses all sorts of ways to save others he has chosen this way to save them. So they offer their lives, living in a community, which is another sort of family, with an Abbot (which is just another way of saying Father) – and discover within that family all the opportunities, joys and alarming discords of family life. And they do that for the sake of all mankind, and above all to the glory of God who gives us all the goal, "You shall be holy, as I am holy." The structure of that family life involves in the first place a shared acceptance of apparent limitations which, when the relation is a true one, are also discovered to be actual liberations – in every sense of the word. To overcome natural distaste because it really is what God wants, is to discover in depth what is meant in scripture by "the liberty of the glory of the children of God". To try and do it for any other reason, and against the will of God, can only lead to inexpressible pain, disillusionment and suffering.

So monks share fellowship with one another in obedience to God but what binds them together is their common search for God. And the most important thing in their lives together is the "Opus Dei", the work of God, the life of prayer.

To that end the last Prior of the Abbey had a whole series of Obligations which he shared with his monks. Day and night they went backwards and forwards in procession from their work to the choir in the Abbey church to pray Mattins, Lauds, Prime, Terce, Sext, None, Vespers, Compline. And to help them there was a whole pile of books, Breviaries, Missals, Psalters, Calendar – until finally they had to have *another* book to tell them how to find their way around!

All these were ruthlessly destroyed as part of the monastic life – the tools of their trade, their life of worship. The new Dean had to make do. But help was at hand.

At that time a brilliant scholar, a theologian, had lodgings in Jesus Lane, close by the friars and among his many gifts was an ability to write the English language. This was Thomas Cranmer. It was he who was largely responsible for answering the Dean's difficulty, by taking that pile of books, all in Latin, and conflating them into one book, which could be available for everyone, the Book of Common Prayer. Of course a lot was left out – but the essentials remained so that there would be a genuine continuity of worship from the old to the new in the Choir of the cathedral – and, of infinite importance, supported by the acknowledgement of that universal Catholic faith as it is understood in our Anglican Church. The pursuit of holiness, men and women still seeking God. The heart of the matter remained even though the monasteries had gone. The ideas of community did not die.

One remarkable effort to revive the spirit of life in community was made by another Cambridge man, Nicholas Ferrar, who in 1625 went with many of his family to live and pray at Little Gidding. Their daily life of prayer and discipline was taken entirely from the Book of Common Prayer. Their life was finally destroyed by the Puritans twenty years later.

During the 18th century, with the notable individual exceptions and the blazing trail of holiness and evangelical zeal of the Wesleys, the Church lapsed into laziness and inactivity. Then revival came. In Cambridge it came through the Evangelical zeal of Charles Simeon who became Rector of Holy Trinity in 1783, and in Oxford a little later by the convergence of three men, Keble, Newman and Pusey, the acknowledged leaders of a Catholic revival – beginning with a return to the full teaching and use of the Prayer Book. They too longed for holiness, and with the revival of sacramental life became convinced that the restoration of the Religious Life was vital to the life of the Church in its wholeness. The return of response to the call of God, the return of the monks and nuns.

And so it was that on Trinity Sunday in 1841 a young woman, Marian Rebecca Hughes, presented herself at the University Church in Oxford to John Henry Newman, dressed in white and wearing an ivory cross. She had been sent by Pusey to receive Communion, having made her promises to God, the first woman to take Religious vows in the Church of England since Henry abolished them almost exactly 300 years before. The first convent of nuns began in 1845, the first community for men in 1866 – and now there are over two thousand monks, friars, nuns, sisters, throughout the Anglican Communion; a recognised part of the Church. Keble, Pusey and Newman faced fierce opposition in their day, and so did the first Religious

Houses – most of that has now disappeared. They perform many tasks – but one thing they have in common with us all – they share both the restlessness and peace of all those who in different ways are seeking God, longing to share his holiness. To that end they face the peril of wearing a habit, living a life which is intended as a sign to God that the search is worthwhile, to the only thing which ultimately makes sense of this life. To this end they need your prayers, that others may hear God calling to share their life which to some will always appear downright odd, perverse – even at times comic.

But then, a favourite text for all Religious comes from St Paul: "We are the impostors who speak the truth."

Sermons For Special Occasions

Confirmation in Ely Cathedral

This person will say I am the Lord's.

Isaiah 44:5

March 1991

SCHINDLER'S ARK – the Booker Prize novel by Thomas Keneally – was published in 1982. It has haunted me since. Now it is an even more haunting film which has a profound effect on every one who sees it – *Schindler's List*. You will know that it is the story of Oskar Schindler, a Nazi supporter, and a big business man, crafty, lusty, a charmer, a speculator, who tricked the Nazi authorities in Poland to save a cross section of Jews from the gas chambers during those years before the end of the war in 1945 known as the Holocaust – the systematic killing of more than six million Jews for no other reason than that they were Jews – men, women and children.

The film pulls no punches. Every horror of the concentration camps, the trains in which people were herded like cattle, the sheer horror of people like us, killing with such cruelty, people like them – and in such vast numbers – left the packed cinema in which I saw it stunned into silence, and the man next to me in unashamed tears.

And Oskar Schindler. Why did he do it? Keneally calls him "a sign of contradiction". This was not the action of a saint, a St Francis of Assisi or Mother Teresa of Calcutta, a specially holy person. But on the contrary, a very worldly man, using every trick in the book to thwart the Nazis. What began in him as an instinctive dislike of the bully and the pervert became a personal campaign against anti-Jewish cruelty – at the constant risk of his own life. So, over the book and the film, hangs the question, *"What instinct drove him to it?"* The answer comes in part from the Jews in the story.

As the war drew to an end and the liberating Russian troops came near to the factory in which the Jewish prisoners worked for Schindler, under his protection, they planned to give him a parting present. It was a ring, made from the gold bridge one of them had pulled out of his mouth. They had engraved on it an inscription from the Talmud, the Jewish scriptures, which read: "He who saves a single soul saves the world entire." As Schindler put it on his finger, he became very solemn. At that moment he realised that they were about to become free – while he became a prisoner. In fact he fled, disguised in prison clothes. Truly "a sign of contradiction".

It is a story of our time. It is happening now in the former Yugoslavia – where it is called "ethnic cleansing". It is a story which reaches the heart of our scriptures, the story of Jesus, who was himself called a sign, and a contradiction.

It is a story which hits us here just because we are here, and all of us being challenged by the contradictions in our own lives. I mean, here in church. This is a very special occasion, a very joyful one, a real party. But it is also very serious. We are here to support – parents, godparents, grandparents, friends – but not all perhaps able to say, as the candidates will; "I turn to Christ" – or, in the words of my text, "I am the Lord's". Some of the congregation, parents, friends, here may even be entertaining a slight sense of contradiction, after all they know the candidates rather well! But we are in good company. St Paul, who never tired of talking about his conversion and commitment to Christ, also called himself "a prisoner of the Lord" – "I am the Lord's", to quote my text, a prisoner, yet free, with a freedom of choice, of action, of love that sprang from Christ himself. But nevertheless choices, sacrifice, pain and joy that can run absolutely contrary to all those who are still prisoners to a wholly human and material view of the world.

To be confirmed might begin only, with an apparently entirely human instinct towards wholeness, identity, justice, in response to unselfishness. Or because cruelty, inhumanity, and the suffering of others must be challenged – or even the simplest, yet most difficult move, to abandon for a moment your security (and the majority avoid it) only to become prisoners to a very human and material view of the world. That was where Oskar Schindler stood at first. Using Jews as slave labour before they were shipped to the gas chambers, he made a killing, a bomb, lots and lots of money. So what instinct changed him to risk his life to save them? It is the same instinct for everyone including you and me – a human instinct, a nudge towards wholeness, justice, compassion – to discover a capacity to abandon the fear of being different, to overcome our self-protection, to be ready to step out of line, do the socially unacceptable thing. And then, if you have the courage to stick with it, in the end to find yourself confronted with the ultimate human contradiction – a Man who saved the whole world by losing his own life.

When Jesus was dying, on a Roman cross, the mockers said, "He saved others – he cannot save himself." But He did, and infinitely more, He showed us, as one of us, how to overcome suffering and pain, and even death itself. To live a life of freedom, to be a very free prisoner, if you like, of joy and peace, and the creative care of other people. To share this life, this vision, is to discover strength to live out the contradictions in our lives as those who say, "I am the Lord's" – not for our own sake, but in the knowledge that "He who saves a single soul, saves the world entire".

The film is in black and white – but there is just one very brief touch of colour. The Jews are being herded into the ghetto, brutally, by the Nazi soldiers. Schindler is watching them from a distance. Among them is a boy, in a red coat, not bright red, just red. He watches this boy, just one in the crowd – briefly the colour appears on the screen – look out for it if you go to see it, and I hope you will, you could easily miss it. Was this boy the "single soul" that led to the instinct of compassion which saved, in the end, nearly two thousand Jews? To respond to such an instinct in our lives – whether we know it or not – is to follow the Jew who died on the cross – "to save the world entire".

The Name of Jesus

ANNUAL ROSE FESTIVAL, WISBECH

The wilderness and the solitary place shall
be glad for them; and the desert shall
blossom and rejoice as the rose.
It shall blossom abundantly and rejoice
even with joy and singing – they shall see
the glory of the Lord and the excellency of
our God.   *Isaiah 35:1*

June 1980

THE desert shall blossom as the rose, it shall blossom
abundantly – well, that's what they always say at the
garden centre or on the seed packet! But I suppose we are
here to celebrate the fact that sometimes, in fact quite often,
the blooms come up to our expectations, and that in them
we see something of the glory of the Lord and the excellency of our God.

When I started thinking about this sermon the first thing
that came to mind was Juliet's lament over Romeo –
"What's in a name? That which we call a rose by any other
name would smell as sweet."

Well, that might be good enough for Romeos - but not for
roses! Growers take great care and delight in the naming of
a rose and the infinite variety of names says something
special about each bloom, and distinctive of the cultivator.
You will have noticed how much those clever men with
perfect gardens on the TV and radio gardening pro-
grammes delight in those tongue-twisting Latin names.

Oh yes, names matter a lot. Think of the arguments over the names for a new baby – and the confusion of the clergyman who has to do the christening. But that is what it is – the *Christ*ening. We become Christians; have a Christian name – the name by which we are known to our family, to the whole world and to God – whether we live up to the promises on the packet or not!

There were never arguments over the name of Jesus. His mother knew before he was born and you could say he was the one Man who came up to expectations in spite of all that life could do to him. So the name of Jesus has a very special place: it reminds us of the possibility of absolute goodness, truth and beauty; reminds us of justice and peace, of hope in a hopeless world, of light in darkness, of health and wholeness for the sick. Above all of kindness, consideration, patience and loving care, of compassion and endurance in the face of pain or despair. It gives courage and faith to those who see only a bleak prospect. The name of Jesus says something too about the overcoming of evil.

In the 12th century there was a good monk called St Bernard who wrote a long hymn praising the name of Jesus. At one time it was known as the Rosy Sequence – as if the name of Jesus was like a marvellous scent – the sweet scent of a perfect rose.

But, you might say, my roses are not always like that. A particular bloom can reach perfection only for a short while, at a particular time on a particular day, and long before that there are endless pests and dangers lying in wait to destroy it.

Another English poet, William Blake, only too well aware of the way Evil can attack all that is good was to write:

Rose thou art sick.
    The invisible worm
That flies in the night
    In the howling storm

Has found out thy bed
　Of Crimson joy
And his dark secret love
　Does thy life destroy.

There is a great mystery in the world – the mystery of suffering. How can it be that God who made such beautiful things, such beautiful people, allows also such misery? While we are celebrating here, the awfulness of Belfast, the bullets, the bombs goes on.

And how do we face the misery of a young police officer who accidentally kills a young and lovely child – they both have Christian names, are known personally to God?

The pathos of his remark, "I will never forget; and his mother will never forgive," must live in our memories: for in lesser ways all our lives have the mixture of terrible pain and wonderful promise. Does it seem as if for all the care in planting, nurturing, feeding and fostering the human life that might grow and bloom into beautiful manhood, womanhood, the cards are stacked against us? Jesus too was only thirty-three when he was wrongfully condemned to a terrifying death.

I believe the answer comes together in Him – the answer that is full of hope, of joy and in the end triumph and peace. That is what He promised. There is a lovely Russian carol which has been set to music by Tchaikovsky called *The Crown of Roses* which tries to describe what I mean:

When Jesus Christ was yet a child
He had a garden small and wild,
Wherein he cherished roses fair
And wove them into garlands there.

Now once, as summertime drew nigh,
There came a troop of children by,
And seeing roses on the tree,
With shouts they plucked them merrily.

"Do you bind roses in your hair,"
They cried in scorn to Jesus there.
The boy said humbly: "Take, I pray,
All but the naked thorns away."

Then of the thorns they made a crown,
And with rough fingers pressed it down,
Till on his forehead fair and young
Red drops of blood like roses sprung.

I know you can grow roses without thorns – perhaps that is what we want to do with life as well.

Jesus took them both – and rose in triumph from death to say to us, "When you are tempted to despair, to feeling that all is lost, when you can only see the dark side of things, your own pain, your own sin, try to remember that the name of Jesus means also victory over death, victory over suffering, the assurance of a life eternal which is yours to enjoy."

I read once a very moving book, the true story of a young and attractive woman who was very severely mentally sick, apparently beyond the point of recovery. She was befriended by someone absolutely determined at all costs and any length to help her back to health. It is the story of a terrible struggle, yet was in the end a triumph. But at the point of despair when the sick girl would have given in, her friend says, "I never promised you a rose garden." And that is the name of the book – *I Never Promised You a Rose Garden*. Lovely as it is you can't live in it all the time, but at its best it can remind us of the promises of God, the promises we celebrate today and which may carry us through another year – for

the desert shall blossom and rejoice as the rose. It shall blossom abundantly and rejoice even with joy and singing . . . they shall see the glory of the Lord and the excellency of our God.

Brecon Jazz Festival

As he approached the house he heard
music and dancing.   *Isaiah 35:1*

*Brecon Cathedral, celebrating the tenth anniversary
of the Brecon Jazz Festival. August 1990*

A FEW months ago I went to buy a new stylus for my
record player. Now, I must be honest and admit I
almost had to rehearse that opening line! I belong to a generation that speaks more readily of wireless than radio, and
gramophone needles than styluses. Which is what happened at the shop. In my confusion I said, "I need a new
needle for my gramophone." To which the bright young
assistant cheerfully replied, "It's for your old 78s, is it
Dad?"

Well, the first gramophone in my family, well over sixty
years ago, was a smart box affair, a portable with a little
fold away handle in front. We also had our pile of old 78s
– Luff singing, "Hear my Prayer", "Tip toe through the
tulips" and Jessie Matthews dancing on the ceiling.
Recently I was reminded on the radio that we had Greta
Keller singing "Mean to Me": but the really great additions
came after I'd heard Sachmo himself at the Brighton
Hippodrome mopping his brow and playing like an angel
during his first visit to England in 1932. I discovered Jazz!

Then suddenly I was given a bunch of songs:
"Summertime and the living is easy"; "Bess you is my
woman now"; "It ain't necessarily so"and "I got plenty of
nuttin" – from then I was hooked on Gershwin, though
I've had to wait for Simon Rattle's recent recording to hear
the whole of that great jazz opera *Porgy and Bess* and the
story of Catfish Row in which it is set.

79

Catfish Row is in the deep South, a small simple fishing community of black people – the world of the Negro spirituals, the world also of cotton picking and slavery. There is fun and laughter – men gamble – and there is sudden drunkenness, violence and murder; then the whole community goes on a gay picnic. There's a fishing tragedy, storm and loss – and the community mourn together. And there's Bess, passed unwillingly from man to man. From the violent murderer Crown to Porgy, whom she loves – and then, when she is deceived into thinking that Porgy is in prison not to return, to the Smart Alec, drug-trafficking Sporting Life, who takes her off to New York. It ends with Porgy setting off to find her – in his goat cart. For Porgy is severely crippled, and suffers the deprivation and sense of rejection known to cripples, of all kinds. Memorably he sings:

> When God made cripple
> he means him to be lonely.
> Night time, day time,
> he got to trabble that lonesome road.

Pervading the whole story is a simple faith, a superstitious faith, a matter of life and death with God looking on. In fact, too simple a faith, too black and white, the sort of faith some old missionaries sometimes seem to preach – the sort of religion that casts God as a God of fear and judgement, without the true compassion and love of a God who understands all too well the frailty of mankind, the complexity of our motives and the blindness of our love. He knows there are emotional and spiritual cripples, moral cripples and mental cripples, and he came and travelled that same lonesome road with them. However, even the faith of Catfish Row is not without its critics: Sporting Life sings, "It ain't necessarily so, the things you are liable to read in the Bible, it ain't necessarily so." In the end, a good deal of it echoes the world of today.

When I first heard those songs I was a boy in the South

London suburb of Clapham – and Clapham then was not so far from Catfish Row – it's all the same, a local community of people sharing love and license and loss. There were picnics and parties, some violence and pain. Many in the community had been crippled by war, others by drink, unemployment or fractured family life. There was loyalty too, and generosity, and longing for freedom – dignity as well as despair. It happens everywhere. After all, it was in London as a boy that I first heard the unemployed miners from the valleys of Wales singing in the streets.

I first met God in my local church – and He was not entirely unlike the God of *Porgy and Bess* – He always knew when I did wrong, but was somehow, it seemed unfairly, looking the other way when I got it right. Well, it ain't necessarily so. And if you'd drawn near the house you would have heard music. Gershwin and the Duke, Django Reinhardt and Charlie Parker. Jazz was the language of life, of love, of longing. It could be also the voice of pain and passion, the language of liberation and freedom, of forgiveness and hope and faith.

Above all Jazz has been our language, the language of this century, yours and mine, the unique musical expression of the common man and woman. It was born when this century began – when incidentally Louis Armstrong was born as well (surely the greatest?). Jazz came of age in the twenties. If you were rich it expressed the abandon of a perpetual party. If you were poor – and millions lived in desperation of unemployment and the dole – the Blues could be the voice of despair.

Just before the Second World War broke out Noel Coward produced a big musical show in London called *Cavalcade* – a sort of revue of the century so far, beginning with the Boer War. In it a disillusioned cabaret singer has a number:

Blues, Twentieth Century blues,
They're getting me down,

Who's escaped these weary
Twentieth Century Blues.
Why, if there's a God in the sky,
Why doesn't he grin,
Up high above this dreary
Twentieth Century din?

When the war came in 1945 – halfway through our ninety years - and divided the men from the boys, the atom
bomb on Hiroshima brought it all to an end. If you were
born after 1945 you have grown up without war – at any
rate in Europe. But you have grown up with the fear of the
appalling consequences of the misuse of nuclear power –
grown up with the misuse of money, of political power,
with the terrifying reality of prisons, refugees, the tyranny
of Communism. In the age now of liberation, of a new
Europe, of the second Prague Spring, of Gorbachev and
Vaclav Havel, we can believe that the old tyrannies that, for
instance, condemned millions of Jews to death, are finally
over. Oh yes, none of those things happened here. Even
Vietnam and the Falklands were a long way off.

But this weekend, suddenly we are faced with the possibility that the century which began with war might end
with war. There is a bigger international force in the
Persian Gulf than at any time anywhere in the world since
1945.

"Why, if there's a God in the sky, why doesn't he grin, up
high above this dreary twentieth century din?" We have
discovered how to do so much, fly faster, see it all as it happens, yet here we are among the cripples again, crippled by
fear, by our dependence on oil, crippled by our uncertainties for the future, shocked by the sudden re-emergence of
another Hitler, another Stalin.

And what is happening on that international scale can be
reflected in our lives, just where we live, in our own
Catfish Row.

My text was taken from a story from Jesus that demonstrates that God is not up there grinning at man's predicament, but down here with us, sharing our lives, as we share His life. It's a story about a man who had two sons (I'm sure he had daughters as well). One went off and lived recklessly until, crippled by poverty, he had the courage to come home and admit he was wrong. His father was thrilled and laid on a big party. The other son who'd always been at home, and inherited the lot anyhow, is also crippled, by jealousy – and though he hears music and dancing, he won't come in. So his Dad has to go out to him as well. His father explains, as he does to us, that in a crippled world the secret of love is forgiveness, learning to live together, trust and generosity, starting again.

That's sometimes a lonely road, but He doesn't sit "up there!" – He's on the road with us, and will be in the days to come. And somehow He makes a party of it. There's music. I wonder what sort? Well, I suppose you will think that because it's God's house it has to be the Bach B Minor Mass. But as a matter of fact I believe that, being God, he has his own special resources, so just for this once he's assembled Miles Davies, and Andy Shepherd, and Oscar Petersen, with a special appearance of Cleo Lane or the old Queen, Ella Fitzgerald, herself!

Come to think of it, anyone passing this house this morning will hear music and dancing, the real celebration of life, because, as I said once before, God is alive and well and living in Brecon – and the Jazz Festival says so. Only don't let it stop here, take it home, for "you are the music while the music lasts". Let it be His music, music that others can hear – music that says above all that He loves you, forgives you, trusts you, for He truly is the King of Jazz.

What is Real?

EPIPHANY AT SANDRINGHAM

They returned home another way

Matt. 2:12

Shortly before the Gulf War. January 1991

TODAY is the twelfth day of Christmas. Dare we look forward after the service to twelve drummers drumming, eleven pipers piping – not to mention ten lords a leaping – but are there partridges in Norfolk?

Today also marks the end of the Christmas season. We call it Epiphany, and remember the Three Wise Men and their even more wonderful gifts. In some parts of Europe this is Christmas, and just as we are finishing they are starting. The children in Spain put out old shoes for gifts in the way we hang up stockings.

Truth to tell, most people by now are a bit tired of Christmas, tired of turkey, and tinsel, tired of all those old films on the telly, and the children are already tired of their new toys.

There's a favourite story for children of all ages about a boy who got tired of his toys. He woke up on Christmas morning to find sticking out of the top of his stocking a fat bunchy rabbit made of velvet, with a sprig of holly between his paws. These days, no doubt, it would have been a Teenage Mutant Ninja Turtle. Well, to begin with he was very pleased with this velveteen rabbit – until more exciting toys came along. And it was abandoned, finally ending up in a cupboard with other forgotten toys.

In the cupboard the rabbit became friendly with the skin

horse, who also, old and battered, had been discarded. Which was as well, because the other toys despised him, particularly the modern mechanical ones who pretended to be real. One day the rabbit said to the horse:

"What is real? Does it mean having things that buzz inside you, and a stick-out handle?"

"Real isn't how you are made", said the horse, "it's a thing that happens to you. When a child loves you for a long, long time, not just to play with, but really loves you, then you become real."

"Does it hurt much?" asked the rabbit.

"Sometimes," said the skin horse, for he was always truthful. "When you are real you don't mind being hurt."

"Does it happen all at once, like being wound up, or bit by bit?"

"It doesn't happen all at once," he replied, "You *become*. It takes a long time. Generally by the time you are real most of your hair has been loved off, and your eyes drop off and you get loose in the joints and very shabby. But those things don't matter because once you are real you can't be ugly except to people who don't understand."

The boy had a Nana, and one night as he was going to bed he couldn't find his favourite toy, and Nana, seeing the toy cupboard open, snatched the rabbit and said, "Take this!" and after that he was never separated from it. Its coat got threadbare, his tail loose, but the boy never noticed. Then one day the rabbit got lost in the garden, but the boy wouldn't sleep until it was found, a very soggy, bedraggled rabbit. Nana grumbled, "Fancy all that fuss for a toy!" But the boy stretched out his hands. "Give me my rabbit", he cried, "he isn't a toy, he's *real*!" and the rabbit was very happy to hear it.

What is real? And more importantly *who is* real? It's a bit difficult to believe those "Personalities" we see on television are real, but that goes for a lot of artificial human situations.

Were the Wise Men real? The centre of the Gospel story is also a boy, Jesus, the most real person who has ever lived, who came to love us into reality. So real that he frightened Herod the King – the Saddam Hussein of his day – into an act of terrible brutality, killing all the Jewish boys of the same age as Jesus, who was then taken into Egypt, a displaced person, a refugee. That was real enough, like the suffering children in Kuwait, the thousands of refugee children all over the world, or the children dying in Africa, threatened by drought and famine on a more terrible scale than ever before.

The point about the Epiphany is that we worship Jesus who didn't just have pity on the human race – He joined it, joined us. We become real as we respond to His love, follow His example.

One of the most real men that I've ever known tried to do that. He was a padre in the First World War sharing the life of men in the mud of the trenches. He returned to find that many of the same men had become an army of unemployed, homeless, often destitute. To help them he joined them. He once said, "If you want to help a man in the gutter, it's no good just putting your hand in your pocket and giving him money. If you really want to help a man in the gutter you must first get into the gutter beside him." And he did just that. It was the beginning of the Franciscan movement in the Church of England, and the establishment of Franciscan houses all over the world, not only for homeless men and women, but for maladjusted boys, the victims of drugs, or AIDS, or anyone, men and women for whom love practically applied might give back their dignity, their reality.

Each morning at our house in Cambridge a little crowd gathers of men who come for tea and sandwiches, some homeless and often hopeless, sadly an increasing number are youngsters with Glasgow or Geordie accents. The

86

problems are not simple – overcrowded or inadequate homes where no-one has a job, violence and rejection. The solutions are not simple, but they too are real people.

As we begin another year those are not the only problems that face our nation; the conflict in Northern Ireland is overshadowed by the greater fear of war as the days before the deadline, January 15th, diminish.

What, in the face of that, can we offer God, as we take our place with the Three Wise Men?

Well, if you would be wise, face the fact that Jesus in his love for us shares our life, even all the ugliness of our lives, and loves us, loves you with beauty, with reality. So offer Him, as a New Year's resolution, a determination to let Him continue to make you the real person He always meant you to be, without fear or anxiety or falsehood – no more pretence. Remember it doesn't happen all at once – it takes time.

Secondly, let Him give you his peace – and make it a principle in your life to be a source of peace and reconciliation in the lives of other people – beginning perhaps with those nearest to you.

And lastly, offer him the intention to find those ways in which you can share the lives of those less fortunate than yourself – there always is someone – whom you might in turn love into reality. That might not be easy – but everyone can do *something*.

Did you read the story, or see it on television, of Angie Hayter, who runs a pub called *The White Hart* near Petersfield? She saw the really terrible pictures of the orphan children in Rumania, shut up in a home without clothes, proper food or even sanitation. She felt she had to do something – so she appealed for help, collected money, clothes, medicines, nappies, blankets – tons of it. The brewers gave her the use of two big lorries, and together with her brother and a few friends, she drove across Europe to see what they could do.

What they saw was more terrible than they could have

87

imagined. But they changed all that. What a gift to God who came as a child and what a very real person! It didn't solve all the problems – but what she did others can do in their own way.

It says of the Three Wise Men that in the face of threat and danger they returned to their home country another way. So may it be for us that in spite of many fears we find the way to face our future with hope, trusting in the reality of the love and peace and strength of God.

Oundle School

Being warned in a dream not to go back to
Herod they returned home another way.

Matt 2:12

January 1991

SITTING in a doctor's waiting room one day last week,
and wondering what I would be saying to you this
morning – the first Sunday of another term, and possibly
the last Sunday of peace in our lives – I was reading some
recent poems by R. S. Thomas. One of them is about the
Three Wise Men. It is quite short:

> The first King was on horseback
> The second a pillion rider
> The third came by plane.

> Where was the God-child?
> He was in the manger
> With the beasts
> All looking the other way –
> Where the fourth was a slow dawning
> Because Wisdom must come on foot.

They had just left Herod, who was the Saddam Hussein
of his day. Seeing Jesus as a rival he murdered all the children of his age in Israel – as Hussein has killed the children
of Kuwait. But Jesus escaped and became a homeless
refugee in Egypt like the millions of refugee children and
victims of mankind all over the world.

So the Wise Men went back another way. Perhaps it took
more time and patience to arrive safely home – but otherwise they might have been killed too.

Well the wise men from the West have been flying in, and Perez de Cuellar, like the fourth wise man, has arrived last – a slow coming. In an hour or two he will be talking to Saddam Hussein – and deserves all our prayers as he tries to find a wiser way than war.

I was born in 1918 in the last year of the First World War – so I remember nothing of it. But I remember the beginning of the Second War only too well. For two reasons.

1939 was a big year for me. In the first place I had my 21st birthday and was given something I'd always wanted – a dog, a wire-haired terrier to be precise, called "Sensational Pete". The most sensational thing about it was that it hated traffic. At the sound of a car or lorry it would sit down firmly and absolutely refuse to budge. I carried that dog an awful lot!

The second thing is that I became a soldier. Neville Chamberlain went to negotiate with Hitler and returned promising "Peace in our time". The crowds were jubilant but they dug trenches in Hyde Park just the same and handed out gas masks.

For the first time for fifty years I have felt during the past week or two the same sense of fearful anticipation of impending disaster. I knew the First War only at second-hand, tales of the trenches where men died, drowned in mud as well as from shells or bullets. As in every home in England there was, on top of the piano, the fading sepia photograph of a favourite uncle, killed on the Somme. At the cinema were flickering, silent newsreels.

In the same way we know something of the Second War. Plenty of graphic movies like *A Bridge too Far*, with plenty of sound. Later still the more horrifying pictures of modern warfare in Vietnam and the Falklands. But since the blinding light, the terrifying instant destruction of 200,000 people in Hiroshima, we have worked towards peace, and even seem to have overcome the Cold War as well. Just a year ago.

But only those over fifty have first-hand knowledge of

the consequences of war. The fear, the crushed senses, the shattered families, the apparent futility, the broken limbs and broken lives, as well as the fierce pride, the heroism, the loyalties of war – and the pity.

Now an international force of a size and power never before assembled in one place, with a capacity to destroy which cannot easily be calculated, and with nuclear resources waiting in the wings – the appalling destructive ability of which we have only glimpsed once many years ago – faces an opponent who with fearsome ruthlessness would not hesitate to escalate a war to include one nation after another regardless of the cost in lives to his own country as well as his opponents.

The Archbishop has urged us to pray today. I need no encouragement – but what in the face of all that do I say, with an apparent deadline on Tuesday.

When I pray I end my prayers as you do, by saying "through Jesus Christ our Lord". Can I rely on that? The prayer takes us back to Bethlehem and those Wise Men – very wise really. They looked at a baby and saw God and believed what they saw, trusted him with their lives.

They saw a baby, a baby like one of us when we were babies, growing up to be a boy the age you are now, like the boy of seventeen, we were told in the press last week, who is the youngest serving soldier in the Gulf, well within the same age range of many of us here. Jesus came to share our lives, be our age, see through our eyes, so that we could see through his. That's what prayer is all about. How does the possibility of war or the path of peace, or the pity war distils, seem to Him? He expressed his solidarity with all mankind, everywhere and at all times, Moslems and Jews as well as Christians, or for that matter those with no faith at all. He lives for all, died for all.

The seventeen-year-old Iraqis have also been called up, thousands of them. Will he have pity on them as well as us?

The point is that Jesus also had his battle with injustice and died as vicious a death as any one in any war. Our presence here this morning asserts our belief that as Man and God He was victorious, that like Him we can find a way of victory over falsehood, injustice, over violence itself. He promised us peace: not that it would be easy, nor peace in the way the world gives peace. But he also adds, "I have overcome the world." If the immediate answer to the terrible dilemmas that face our wise man this weekend seem unanswerable, it is not so for God. So we can pray with confidence to see as He sees, praying that His will be done on earth as it is in heaven, and for a peace which may pass our understanding, but not his. Then we might be like the Wise Men, look into the face of God and find our peace, not with Herod or Hussein but with Him, and set our feet to return home another way.

Consecration of the Bishop in Europe in St Paul's Cathedral

– AND THE DAY ON WHICH THE DESERT WAR WAS DECLARED

After breakfast Jesus said to Simon Peter,
"Simon son of John do you love me more
than all else?" *John 21:15*

January 17, 1991

IT seems almost uncannily appropriate that on this first morning of another war, we should meet here on the Feast Day of St Anthony who fled from the world to find peace and prayer – find God – in the desert. May he and all the saints pray with us and for us as we embark on the first day of a changed world. Peter also woke up to a new day that would change his life.

It was after the death and resurrection of Jesus, but before they really knew and entirely accepted that He had risen from the dead. Peter, James and John went fishing all night and caught nothing. Then in the early morning light they see a stranger on the shore, who shouts out to them, calls them friends, directs them to where they can throw their nets for a certain catch.

Suddenly there is a moment of recognition and John cries from his own heart's love, "It is the Lord!" While Peter just plunges impetuously over the side to be the first at the shore, as he was the first at the tomb. There Jesus has arranged a meal – breakfast – fresh fish cooked on a small fire. He gives thanks and they sit and eat. Once more He is at the head of the table, their Master and Lord. He is at the head of the table as He had been in the Upper Room. So much has happened – between the Last Supper and the First Breakfast. Their whole world has changed – and for Peter, hanging over the meal is a harsh reality.

How can Jesus eat with a man who deserted him at the time of his greatest need, denied violently that he had ever known him, even though he had once boasted that if necessary he would die for him? Do you say, "Oh forget it, I know you didn't mean it, it could happen to anyone." Pretend it never happened. Not so with Jesus. So in the embarrassing silence he asks a question. "Simon, son of John, do you love me more than all else?". Not just "Simon do you love me?", but as in the New English Bible, "Simon son of John, do you love me *more than all else*?"

Peter looks up, "So, he thinks I am no longer Peter the rock, the chosen foundation stone for the Church – now I am right back at square one where I started, and just Simon again."

Jesus goes on asking him not once or twice but three times. Peter is no fool, he can count up to three, that was the number of times he denied Jesus, so he is almost in despair to reply.

After His death on the cross there was for Peter – for all of us – no question of the nature and depth of the love of Jesus, its quality, its perfection. "He died that we might be forgiven." "Will you love me", he says to Peter, "with the love with which I have loved you?" With a love that establishes forgiveness as the ultimate visible sign of love in the world. That is His challenge to us all, that is what must be seen to be the hallmark of our ministry. To be forgiven and accept the love of Jesus and love Him in return, above all else. Above ambition or success, above the favour of men, above money, above even the proper gifts of family or other friends – not that you love them less because you love Him more. Love Him, not as prelates in palaces, but as penitents among the people. "Lord you know that I love you!" To love Him like that is to liberate new initiatives of reconciliation into the world, even as it was liberated in the life of Peter. Not only in the familiar places of broken homes, broken marriages, broken parishes, divided Churches, but critically in the coming years in our own Church as we face the possibility of division over the Ministry. After all, will you be present to assist at the consecration of the first woman bishop in St Paul's?

Above all, this very day; from a heart of love, and with the authority of Christ to speak on His behalf, we are called to reconcile the use of the most terrifying and sophisticated weapons of war, with a capacity to destroy human lives never known before, with His principles of peace and reconciling love. In the face of such a challenge I find myself saying with Peter, "Lord you know all things" – and pray for His peace with His people. But there was another practical demonstration of the same love contained in the question. The New English Bible also suggests that the third time Jesus asked the question he said not "Do you love me?" but *"Are you my friend? Are you?"* There is no question of all that friendship meant to Jesus. He spelt it out before he died. "Greater love has no man than this, that a man lay down his life for his friends." Then he was killed. Now he says to Peter, "Are you my friend?" Peter was to prove his friendship by dying for Jesus as countless others have done since, and there are many others in the conflicts of this present world, who live out their lives in radical uncompromising friendship for the Kingdom of Heaven's sake. Friendship with God it was called by St Aelred; St Ignatius, founder of the Jesuits, called his first company of followers "Friends in the Lord", and our much respected and loved Quakers are more properly known as "The Religious Society of Friends".

As bishops and pastors, can we offer less than a profound love of God in a ministry of friendship which rejoices in all that makes us different socially, sexually, spiritually, racially? A friendship that is radical in this

95

recognition of our common likeness to Christ, and that can surmount all the barriers of class, culture or creed.

It may be that very soon, now that words have given way to wars, Christians, Moslems and Jews will all find themselves in conflict. May the day come when faith becomes a foundation of peace as we acknowledge that we all have the same spiritual father in Abraham, who was recognised as the friend of God.

And finally there is the commission, "Feed my sheep", and he offers the food himself. So we are once more in the familiar world of the family meal – getting our feet under the table, sharing in a meal which is also a foretaste of the Heavenly Banquet. There is a practical consequence to his command, "Come and eat". It is hard to feast and fight at the same time. So we come to this meal where we feed on His body and blood, share in the mystery of His loving sacrifice and are made one with the offering he makes for us, for ever in heaven.

We are called also to feed ourselves, and claim the imperative to feed the people by the proclamation of the Good News of the Gospel, and not least during the coming ten years.

I have sometimes heard the Decade of Evangelism described in ways that suggest that as the year 2000 dawns we shall all heave a sigh of relief and say "Thank goodness that is over, now we can get back to work!" It is as well to remember that as he entrusts you today as bishops, to feed His people by declaring His love, His forgiveness, His friendship and His heavenly food, so we are also commissioned to "show forth the Lord's death, and life – till He comes – finding in Him our confidence and peace.

Edinburgh Festival

But there is somewhere a solemn assurance
which runs: "What is man, that thou
rememberest him, or the son of man, that
thou hast regard to him? Thou didst make
him for a short while lower than the
angels; thou didst crown him with glory
and honour."   *Hebrews 2:6-7*

St Mary's Episcopal Cathedral, Edinburgh,
during the Edinburgh Festival. August 1994

THERE is a poem by Browning, "Soliloquy of the
Spanish Cloister", about a disgruntled monk who cannot stand a fellow monk – the gardener! It begins:

> Grrr -there go, my heart's abhorrence,
> Water your damned flowerpots do!
> If hate killed men, Brother Lawrence,
> God's blood, would not mine kill you!

It aptly illustrated one major test of the Religious Life –
the other monks, or nuns, as the case may be.

Franciscan friars often find themselves living in small
numbers in small houses with small rooms. You get to
know each other, day in day out rather well – particularly
each other's idiosyncrasies, eccentricities, peculiarities and
oddities. Well for the past eight years I have had the same
brother living in the room just above me. "He knows," as
the Psalmist says, "my goings out and my comings in." We
have survived as brothers and friends because we share
some of the same interests, and not least our love of music,
though sometimes in our cramped quarters we suffer from
what might be called "CD rivalry"! He has a taste for late

97

Schönberg and Tippett – but is, deplorably, quite unable to appreciate jazz! *I* can never remember who wrote what – he has the awful habit of singing along with whatever he is listening to. And he has his enthusiasms. Recently he had wall-to-wall Mahler on all day long – and very loud. Oddly enough it did me a good turn. I was sitting underneath trying to reply to a letter from the Provost and wondering what to preach about when I remembered that somewhere I had heard on the radio the "programme" around which Mahler wrote his Third Symphony – as I later discovered, in August 1895, almost exactly a hundred years ago.

He was sitting in his country retreat in Austria – with a meadow full of flowers sweeping down almost to his window. And in distress. His brother had committed suicide, he was conscious of his constant rejection as a Jew and his health was bad. He was also deeply aware of the world as a place of struggling, suffering humanity. Well, that is also our world today: a world of inescapable sickness and the misuse of power; of Bosnia and Rwanda; a world of racial and religious discrimination; of poverty and unemployment. Much of that struggle had been reflected in his first two symphonies. Now he looked out as if asking Creation for an answer to questions which are as much with us as they were with him and from which there is no escape even in the middle of a great Festival of Music like this one. So he asked himself, "What do the flowers of the meadow tell me?" It was the moment of inspiration for which he had been looking. It became the title of the first movement of the new work. Then he heard far off the melancholy bells the cattle wear and fresh titles followed. "What do the morning bells tell me?" "What does the cuckoo tell me?" A child came in view: "What does the child tell me?" More were added until the whole enormous Third Symphony had come to mind . . . a gigantic hymn to the glory of every aspect of Creation – echoing in music the language of St Francis himself.

Of all the titles Mahler considered there were three that

had stuck in my mind. "What man tells me"; "What the angels tell me"; "What Love tells me"; and Bruno Walter, who as a very young student was the first to hear it, communicated, "Night speaks of Man, the morning bells speak of Angels, Love speaks of God."

In my text the writer of the Epistle to the Hebrews says, "What is man that thou art mindful of him, or the son of man that you had a regard for him? You made him a little lower than the angels to crown him with glory and power."

Summer is the season of music festivals. Those I know best are the Jazz Festival in South Wales and the very English Three Choirs, founded over 250 years ago. But unquestionably the greatest is here in Scotland. They all have this in common, that they hold up a mirror to humanity made, like Jesus, a little lower than the angels, caught up in the crudity and chaos of Creation as well as its infinitely complex glory; our world of Bosnia and Rwanda, of violent death on our doorsteps in Ireland; of a world where a good seat at the opera here would feed a family for a week or a month in the Third World; of AIDS and unemployment.

It sounds almost cynical to say, "What is man that you have regard for him?", or ask with Mahler, "What does Man tell me?" It depends which man or woman is speaking – Bill Clinton or Virginia Bottomley; a priest or a politician, a princess, a public personality, or the latest victim of publicity in the popular press. Mahler as a Jew suffered from racial and religious discrimination. Beethoven, whose late sonatas moved me to tears this week, wrote them when he was almost stone deaf and could hear only the hidden voice. Both of them tell me there is hope. That mankind is not condemned to disaster. I hear it too in the sublime golden trumpet of the late Miles Davies – the voice of a suffering first known in a particular way by black people living as slaves in a white world and giving us a unique musical idiom with which to express the desolation of man's misuse of power in this century. Yet jazz also celebrates deliverance from slavery. It can also be, like Bach or Beethoven, the voice of the one man whose birth into the world gives hope to all humanity, the voice of Jesus.

If you doubt that, then listen to the angels. I don't mean those dreadful androgynous, insipid non-beings, so loved by the pre-Raphaelites. If you want to come to grips with angels then beg, borrow or steal a ticket for Newman and Elgar's *Dream of Gerontius*, the inspired climax of this Festival. The angels there are as mighty as an army with banners.

Angels are God's way of speaking directly to us. You may find the conventional God of the Christians beyond belief. Then suspend for a moment your disbelief and allow the hidden language of this service to speak to you, the language of the heart, the language of Love. It comes disguised in the mock gothic grandeur of a great building and the music of Mozart. Don't be deceived. It is the language of all humanity, of Love, and that means suffering and pain and loss – and your own particular pain, whatever it might be, in with all the rest. It is about bread and wine – flesh and blood; the language of a man who for the love of each one of us paid the highest price of death to give us a new assurance, a new hope, the capacity to forgive and be forgiven and start again. What he said was, "Greater love has no man than this, that he lay down his life for his friends – you are my friends."

That is what Love tells me, tells you – not that it is the only thing, but the supreme expression of unselfishness, generosity, freedom – something I can say to others, and so can you.

This is the music of Love. "Music," says Eliot, "heard so deeply that it is not heard at all – but you are the music while the music lasts."

So for you the Festival could be the rediscovery of a music, a voice, for future days: days which may be clouded with uncertainty, pain, or loss, or no less filled with confidence, peace, joy. A voice reassuring, strengthening, comforting you.

For you the Festival need never be over, because it is here you came to know: "What Man tells me"; "What the Angels tell me"; and "What Love tells me".

Profession of the First Two Brothers at Burford Priory

When the Lord saw that Moses had turned aside to look, He called to him out of the bush, "Moses, Moses," and Moses answered, "Yes, I am here."   *Exodus 3:4*

The Priory of Our Lady, Burford, Oxfordshire.
The Priory Chapel has a large carving of the Burning Bush over the door. May 1st, 1989

I T may not come as a complete surprise to some of you that I have chosen a text from this particular story. The carving on the chapel suggests a local link with a tradition of prayer older even than the stones of the Priory.

This story, the key to the vocation of Moses, opens also a door through which we may glimpse some vision, gain some understanding, of the mystery which is the vocation of every Religious – and not least those whose lives we are sharing here.

Moses had fled from his own country and become, as he said, an alien in a foreign land. He married a local girl and settled down as a shepherd, looking after the sheep of his father-in-law.

In a barren land he is drawn towards Mount Horeb, later to be identified as the Holy Mountain, the Mountain of God, the place of God's Presence. So, on an apparently ordinary day, it began for him.

And we are all drawn, instinctively perhaps, intuitively, almost unknowingly, drawn in a thousand different ways; drawn in circumstances so natural as to be unnoticed, drawn possibly by nothing so clear as "the voice of his calling". Drawn from responsibilities, from conscious and known needs; drawn from the reassuring world of such security as we know, that world which conforms to patterns of life in which, no doubt, we have already excelled in some degree.

Drawn, above all, from a world which questions – why? A question which finds an echo in our own heart, even though the same heart has, in the words of Wesley, been "strangely warmed", as if we had been drawn "by the cords of a man and with bands of love", as Hosea puts it. And all we can answer is, "I saw a bush burning." "A *bush burning*"? – it defies credibility.

But what is incredible to man is inevitable with God. If we make but the first move, the first response to His love, then for us the exchange of love is unique, for you alone. Drawn by His love, and almost unawares, responding to it, the first warm breath can seem like a consuming fire, which is what some friendly observers might naturally see. After all, they were not there, they hadn't *seen* the bush blazing. "It's all very well to be a bit religious. I sometimes go to the early service myself – but to be a monk – that's completely over the top." "Religious fervour is one thing – religious fever is another – but don't worry, perhaps it will burn itself out."

But Moses replies, and we reply with him, "I must go and see this wonderful sight, why does not the bush burn away?"

I once heard the great and holy Dr Archie Craig, a sort of Scottish Michael Ramsey, preach with great power on this text. It is over thirty years ago, but I remember it as yesterday – "It was only a wee bush, but it *went on burning*." So Moses *had* to go and see.

Moses, it says, "*turned aside*". It could, you might say, have only been curiosity – but then God is like that. He will use every instinct in us to draw us to himself. We know also that for Moses it was also the restlessness of an alien, the distant cry of his own captive people – and anyhow, the

103

bush *didn't* burn away, as the instinct which draws us to God just *won't* die down.

So he left his sheep, as we appear to leave parents and families, friends, parishes, banks and colleges, careers, homes and all the safe structures; drawn into the incomprehensible mystery of God.

It is very hard for others, for those who love us, to see us turn aside. As children we were always warned not to go too near the fire – and now they can do nothing to stop us.

And there was nothing to stop Moses. Humanly speaking that first step of his conformed to the whole eternal purpose of God for mankind. Just that. The whole future of the people of Israel, the redemption of God's people, even our presence here, appears to depend as much on that moment on the Holy Mountain when Moses turned aside from his work and towards God, as it later depended on Mary as she replied to his Angel, "Be it unto me according to thy word." There is a golden thread of obedience to God which leads from that first step towards the unconsuming fire, to the ground on which we are standing now.

And it is only then and there that God speaks at last, calling him by name. "Moses, Moses." It is hard to understand why some people are called to this life rather than others. Called, as if personally – by name. Called, as if only in that way they will find fulfilment, purpose, happiness in life. We live in a world where a great many people are not happy or fulfilled, not really themselves, because they never found the right niche, never did the work they know themselves "cut out for". (It is a happy by-product of early retirement that an increasing number of men and women are being given a second chance these days.)

For Moses, as for the Psalmist, it was the "today" of conviction, you might almost say of conversion. "Today if you will hear his voice."

"Take off your sandals," says God, "the place where you are standing is holy ground."

Why, we might ask, *this* place? Why *Burford*? Is this our

Horeb? Nothing with God is merely accidental. This place can have as much meaning for us as Jerusalem for David, Subiaco for Benedict or La Verna for Francis. There are places where the spiritual air is thin, where the glimpses of goodness are possible, where the glory and radiance of God break through and the powers of love pour out with such brightness that this world seems in comparison shadowy, insubstantial, grey. Places where men "have trod, have trod, have trod". God's meeting places, where He is always waiting for us. It is Jordans for the Quakers and Wesley's Chapel in Bristol for Methodists, and for a thousand years God has been meeting with monks at Bec and Canterbury, Durham and – for many hundreds of years – here. The places only for those who are truly called to be here, for sisters and brothers, the place where the holy becomes home, the natural place to be.

And that is the way it is. God says, "Moses, Moses," and he replies, "Here am I."

Much of the life of a priory is quite simply the echo of that "Here am I". So much of what is called the Spiritual Life is an endless extension and penetration of that response, "Here am I". The religious promise of stability is not an arbitrary discipline, but a glad affirmation that we have found the place of His presence for us, a place where prayer and work, and prayer and pleasure may be one. And if that is reassuring for those who live here, it can in time be as reassuring for those who don't.

Just to know they are there, where the voice of God can be heard, where it is not blotted out by the clamour and confusion, the turmoil and terror of this world. It is no wonder that St Benedict had such a concern for guests. He knew that men and women of all kinds would turn instinctively to the holy mountain in times of distress, or just for the perspective made possible by the lives of men and women who *make* it possible by living there – all the time. No market forces, cost effectiveness or monetarist policies

105

could ever calculate in the currency of peace and reconciliation the value of such places of prayer.

There is a brief and touching epilogue. Moses, it says, "covered his face, for he was afraid to gaze on God." It was for him as for the brothers here, all four of them now, and the sisters who have been here so long, only the beginning. Learning how to live with the glory of God is truly a matter for fear, for the proper awe, which is so much more than mere reverence. We know that, only too well. The trouble is that He invites us so intimately into His world – the joy is that we begin to discover how to live in it.

Years later the day came for Moses, when he climbed up into the mountain, into the very presence of God, that when he returned there were others who covered *his* face, for it glowed so brightly with God's own glory. And so shall all our lives be changed if, according to the path he has given us, we are faithful, changed "from glory into glory"; for "we shall see him, as he is."

The Indignation of Jesus

ST LUKE'S DAY

Once he was approached by a leper, who
knelt before him begging his help. "If you
will", said the man, "you can cleanse me."
In warm indignation Jesus stretched out
his hand, touched him, and said, "Indeed I
will; be clean again."   *Mark 1:40-41*

Little St Mary's Cambridge. October 18, 1992

L IKE many people today I have friends who are suffering from, or have died of AIDS. Not of course that it is
always talked about. Fear, anxiety, distaste and mostly
embarrassment prevent that: "well after all, you know how
it's caught" and, "well, I did not know he was like
that."And in spite of all the publicity to the contrary, "Well,
it is catching isn't it?" Compassion? "Oh yes, we're *terribly*
sorry." And there's no cure, so you are facing a young man
(they are usually young) with the marks of certain death on
him. "And I know we're all Christians, but there *is* a
problem about drinking from the same chalice, isn't there –
even if it is the Blood of Christ?" But what would *He* say
about it? That is spelt out exactly in this text.

There is no question in the mind of Mark when he told
the story of Jesus in the Gospel. From the time He began to
fulfil his vocation Jesus did two things. Firstly He told
everyone about the new world He had come to establish.
He called it the Kingdom of Heaven, an eternal Kingdom
in contrast to the kingdoms of this world – a new way of
looking at the whole of life. And secondly he made clear
the radical change that can come into the lives of those who

live by his teaching. The first time he speaks out in the synagogue everyone is impressed deeply by his preaching and teaching, but also by the power he exercises to heal the sick, give the mentally ill their sanity, make people whole – a valid sign, readily understood, of a spiritually and physically sane world. All sorts are helped, Peter's mother-in-law, crowds who are brought to him in the evening – and one man who came of his own accord, this leper, this outcast, a mass of distorted limbs and open sores, condemned to live outside the city, untouchable, ceremonially unclean, with the signs of Death on him; who always saw the look of fear in the eyes of those who came too near, something which sufferers from AIDS know so well. He comes to Jesus and says, "If you wanted to you could make me clean. Heal me – even me!" And, it says, "In warm indignation Jesus replied, 'of course I want to. Be clean'." But there is more to it than that, much more. He reached out his hand and *touched* him. He didn't just heal him, He went over to his side, made Himself one with him – one with the outcast, the untouchables, which from the point of view of the religious authorities was scandalous. And he was healed.

Nothing could more graphically illustrate His teaching about the Kingdom. In Jesus we see God taking action to save us all, in the only way he can, by coming into the world as one of us – not just healing us from a distance, as it were, but by coming over to our side to heal and restore us: not merely from our physical pains, but even more from our chronic failure, the sickness of humanity we call selfishness, self-centredness – or briefly, sin. Not sin as a string of peccadilloes, but sin as an all encompassing alienation from God and his intention for us. So it says of Jesus, that, "He made himself sin for us, He who knew no sin." In the end He knew what sin can do – He became the ultimate outcast, untouchable, dying as a criminal, deserted by friends, from fear – that we might know what lies beyond death – the terminal condition common to us all.

So Jesus reaches out to each one of us in our untouch-ability to heal us, make us whole, welcome us with the words of His love, sharing His life, His values, coming over to our side that we might live on His – and suffering from the rulers of this world some of the consequences.

Today is St Luke's Day. We honour the Beloved Physician, as he was called by St Paul. Well, there have been, still are, beloved physicians in my life at Addenbrooke's and Papworth who keep me going, and I pray for them and thank God that through them the phys-ically healing work of Jesus still goes on. I imagine it is much the same for many of you. But I equally value the godly priests and pastors in my life who have helped in the healing of my soul, and given me the assurance of God's forgiveness – have helped to drive out the devils of despair, the consequences of selfishness and sin – a healing every bit as real.

It is also the Sunday set apart to pray for the Health Service. In those heady years just after the Second World War, as we began to implement the Beveridge Plan, "put in place" – to use the phrase much loved by our present politi-cians – the Welfare State, it seemed a bit like the coming of the Kingdom of Heaven. Free medical treatment for all, better schools, provision for old age, comparatively little unemployment. And for a while it almost happened. Well they got some of their calculations wrong. But what have we now? Three million unemployed, St Thomas' Hospital – the beloved physician that helped to save my life and familiar friend to countless South Londoners, a centre of excellence – threatened with closure, with three more, all used by God in discovering new ways of healing.

But this Sunday may also survive with another title – Pit Closure Sunday. Cannot we sense the warm indignation of God, as he sees a nation spinning off course and out of control because it puts money before men, suffering from a monstrous sickness that cripples and distorts the lives of millions. A shipyard worker said to me, "Close the shipyard and you might as well cut off my hands." But they shut the shipyards just the same. It is equally true of the mines – and the miners, whole villages condemned to a terminal illness, the signs of which embarrass us, unable to meet the eyes of these new lepers.

So where do we go from here? We all know only too well our own sicknesses, our untouchability. In this service we can bring our need, and the needs of our nation, to the most beloved Physician of all – saying, "If you will, you can make me clean," – share his indignation over the treatment of the nurses and doctors, the mining community and all the unemployed, and pray for a healing of mankind, for the healing power of the political, the distribution of wealth, the restoration of dignity, the longing for justice, the manifestation of love, care and compassion – and the recognition of those values which Jesus called the Kingdom of Heaven.

And if, when you pray, you find yourself filled with warm indignation, don't worry, you're absolutely right – so was He.

The Light of the World

A MEDITATION
LUMEN CHRISTI – THE
LIGHT OF CHRIST

God said, "Let there be light."
Jesus said, "*I* am the Light."
Paul said, "Walk as children of light."
The light shines in the darkness, the
darkness of the world – of our own lives.
Jesus says, "I am the light of the World."
Jesus came to dispel our darkness.

Portsmouth Cathedral: Gathering for
2,000 Young People. June 1989

IN St Paul's Cathedral there is a picture sometimes dismissed as Victorian, but now being appreciated more
and more. It is called *The Light of the World.* We've seen it
all over the place – look at it again. The colours are sombre,
yet they glow. It is night. Jesus, the risen Jesus, stands in
majesty, yet still wearing the signs of his Passion. In one
hand is a lantern, a light. With the other he is knocking on
a door. The picture illustrates another word from scripture.
"Behold I stand at the door and knock. If anyone hears my
voice and opens the door I will come in and sup with him
and he with me."

So the Majesty is standing at the door. It clearly hasn't
been opened for a long time – there are weeds and
brambles round it.

And another thing if you look closely, there is no handle
on the outside, it can only be opened from the inside. If you

want to, you can let him in, the choice always yours – though He makes the first move. He knocks on the door, the personal door of the lives of each one of us, of mine, of yours. For whatever reason you think you have come here, one thing is certain; you are here because God wanted you here. He is the reason you are here – He was waiting for you, drew you, with the voice of His calling. Jesus says, "If anyone hears my voice and opens the door."

I can pretend I haven't heard – no-one else will ever know. I've heard it all before – there's nothing new here – it was better at Taizé.

Yet there is something you can do – I can do – to open the door and let Him into my life in a new way.

And suddenly, He is there and in the brilliant light of His love the furniture of my life looks a bit different but some-how smudgy. Even downright wrong.

He holds out His hand and says, "The keys." He goes everywhere – even the kitchen. Funny, did He know I was faddy about food, or just plain greedy, that light He's still carrying seems to show everything up.

Finally, He searches "my" room. "God, I'd forgotten what a mess I've left it in." And God holding up His light shows that it's worse even than I thought.

What a mess, what confusion. My books – I hope He can't see the one meant to be tucked out of sight. My diary – so many promises unfulfilled. My word processor – but He *is* the Word – oh the terrible misuse of words, conceited, selfish, cruel, opinionated, and so often not quite true or downright lies – and so He looks round. The pic-tures – my parents who never really understand me – but have I really tried to understand them? The friends I chose, and the friends who chose me, forget me. But this is what He sees in the   relentless light of His love. "You are *my* friends." "I have chosen you."

Suddenly, He's trying the door of a corner cupboard. "It's locked." "Yes, sorry, I mislaid the key a long time ago." But with Him nothing is lost – and finally it's open. And there they are. All the things I tried to hide, tried to forget. The occasions of guilt, of shame, the relics of past selfishness – so much I'd rather not remember. The light seems stronger than ever. On the table is the stub of my cheque book, so many made out to self. I

turn away from it and suddenly I catch a glimpse of myself in the mirror, standing beside Him – seeing myself as He really sees me, with love and pity in His eyes, seeing what I might be – seeing what I am. And I do what I've done before on the rather threadbare carpet – I kneel, I want to hide my face – but my eyes are now just on the level of His hand – and it has a deep scar in the middle of it. The light breaks through. So that's what He meant, "Greater love has no man than this, to lay down his life for his friends." The light almost seems to burn – I also remember He said, "Father forgive them – they don't know what they are doing." Well, I do now – and so does He – there are no words for this – only His.

And then He does what I can't do for myself – He lifts me up – with that same hand to stand, side by side with Him again. Saviour – He is risen, for me.

And then an astonishing thing happens. He hands me His light. He hands me His light and says:

"Now – let your light so shine before men that they may see your good works and glorify your father which is in heaven."

"Let your light shine."

"Walk as children of Light."

The Pain of God

Simeon blessed them and said to Mary his mother, "This child is destined to be a sign which men reject; and you too shall be pierced to the heart."   *Luke 2:34,35*

May Day: Ely Cathedral. Sunday, 1st May, 1994

THOSE of my friends who know me well mock me a little for my enthusiasm for the Cinema. Well, there are three films showing at present, all exceptionally good and nominated for Oscars, and all trying to say something hopeful about suffering – the sort of human suffering we know and understand both at a personal as well as a universal level.

Schindler's List is about the Holocaust – the deliberate extermination of six million Jews. Well, that sort of horror is with us now in the slaughter of Moslems, ethnic cleansing, Rwanda, or even on our own doorstep in Northern Ireland, almost every day.

Then there is the moving personal story of C. S. Lewis in *Shadowlands* about the death of his wife from cancer so soon after their marriage. This great scholar, overwhelmed with confusion of personal pain and grief – and for so universal a cause, something we all know.

Another film, *Philadelphia*, described in painful detail the fight for justice for a young man dying with AIDS. Very personal, yet again universal, with millions throughout the world who are HIV positive.

I watched that with particular concern. This time next week I will be in Lourdes leading a party of sixty men, women and children with HIV or AIDS, and their supporters. All three films were nominated for Oscars – but no

114

prizes were offered for answers to the question which hangs over them, spelled out in the heart-rending cries of C. S. Lewis.

They all offer signs of hope – and the hope, like the terrifying question of human suffering, is a human sign.

"Where, God, are you in all this? Why do you permit this?" The suffering we inflict on each other, the pain, the destruction of body, mind and spirit for those who suffer, and those who wait, and watch and weep.

Why these appalling, universal, unanswerable and destroying diseases?

Films are so frequently a reflection not only of life, but of the unconscious longing and needs of those who go to see them. And it is not only the Christians who ask the questions. For the others there is also the problem that the Christians do not appear to know the answers either.

Well, faced with the pictures of a man shot dead in front of his wife in Belfast; the children who will die of AIDS who I am taking to Lourdes this week; or the latest news from Bosnia and Rwanda it might seem far fetched to say that Jesus is giving us an answer when he replies to Philip's question by saying, "Anyone who has seen me has seen the Father."

It is the first of May – Maypoles and dancing in the aisles, at any rate at Thaxted – Morris dancing that is!

Gerard Manley Hopkins reminds us, "May is Mary's month". "Why fasten upon her. With a feasting in her honour?" Well, he goes on and says why in many lovely verses about Spring:

> All things rising all things sizing
> Mary sees, sympathising
> With that world of good
> Nature's Motherhood.

and concludes:

This ecstasy all through mothering earth
Tells Mary her mirth till Christ's birth,
To remember and exultation
In God who was her salvation.

Mary brings the questions about suffering and pain very close to us. She suffered misunderstanding from her neighbour, the pain of childbirth itself, but also a prediction that there was more to follow, "A sword shall pierce your heart also." All mothers suffer in the suffering of their sons and daughters. How could it be otherwise, when it is they who gave themselves for their life?

A mother once said to me, "My son has become a stranger to me." That was her pain. Could that have ever been the case between Mary and Jesus?

Jesus had said, "Blessed are the pure in heart for they shall see God." Of all humanity Mary qualifies as "pure in heart" – absolutely. When she looked at her grown Son what did she see? Flesh of her flesh certainly, but more. He too was pure in heart. As heart speaks to heart – did she see God? I don't mean, did she kiss her son and say, "Good morning God"? But did she know in her heart unspokenly, that if he had said to her, rather than to Philip, "He who has seen me has seen the Father," the instincts which lie beyond human love would have answered, "Yes, I know." The question is important for us, because she *is* one of us – for all her beauty, goodness and truth. So if it is possible for her it is possible for me; even if the possibility seems pretty remote.

And if that is true – then as she watched her God-Son suffer and die, the sword struck fiercely through her heart also, as it does through the heart of every mother who watches a son or brother, husband or friend, all humanity, caught up in a suffering and pain which is both ours, and His. God's suffering for God's world, God suffering with and in God's world.

In our humanity we rightly cry – for him, for ourselves –

116

this is unfair, undeserved, beyond reason, against all idea of a God of Love. Until we begin to see the pain in the face of the Father and not just the pain in the face of the Mother who is Mary. So it is our humanity which can lead us to God, to see Him. I quote: "If in the face of every man and woman we can recognise the face of Christ the Son of Man, and if in the face of Christ we can recognise the race of the Heavenly Father, our humanism can also declare that to know God one must know Man." It comes from a speech by Pope Paul V. And I got it from a book about Pierre Teilhard de Chardin, a great Jesuit scholar and man of prayer who believed passionately in the human race made in the image of God; but also saw the fulfilment of which this resurrection season of spring is a promise. And the signs are always there – in *Schindler's List*, for all its pain, in Oskar Schindler who, at the risk of his own life, saved hundreds from the gas chambers; in the struggle of a scholar like C. S. Lewis with his own personal problem of pain, and his capacity to enter into that dark night with Jesus and finally give hope in his writing to countless others; in the fiercely antagonistic black lawyer in the film, whose fears were overcome in a fight for justice and care for those who suffered with AIDS.

Like the bursting of the trees in May, which is Mary's month, we can look into the face of other men and women and begin the process of purity of heart which may lead us finally to see God the Father in the face of Jesus Christ, His Son our Lord.

And looking into His face we find that our pain is one with the pain of God, as His entire creation moves towards wholeness in hope and peace. And beyond the pain, beyond even the worst of the suffering there in all its horror, universally, personally (and we cannot pretend otherwise) is the certainty of Love, renewing, restoring, recreating us, for we have seen that also – in the face of the Father.

Witnesses to
the Word

Mahatma Gandhi and
C. F. Andrews

THE IMPACT OF MAHATMA
GANDHI
ON C. F. ANDREWS

*King's College, Cambridge at a seminar to celebrate
the centenary of Gandhi. October 1994*

WHEN Mahatma Gandhi came to England for the
round table conference in 1931 he found time to visit
Cambridge, staying with the then Master of Pembroke. The
London policeman who had travelled everywhere with
him since his arrival is said to have remarked before they
left, "Mr Gandhi is very wonderful man."

He was persuaded to come here by another rather wonderful man – Charles Freer Andrews, C.F., or 'Charlie' to
his friends, of which he had a countless number. C. F.
Andrews had been an undergraduate at Pembroke, and
later in life made it a home from home when on leave from
India.

In 1904 he went to India, in the first place as a missionary sent out and supported by an English missionary
society, and for a while taught in a mission school, St
Stephen's College, Delhi. But the more he travelled in India
as a missionary of the Society for the Propagation of the
Gospel, the more stifled he felt by the weight of Anglican
tradition which governed all church life in India. He had
hoped that in Christ the people of India would find the
fruition of their newly discovered national hopes and
dreams. But he discovered that the Indian Church, because
it was not truly Indian, could never fulfil that hope. Ten
years after his arrival in India, as he began to see everything through Indian eyes, he abandoned any idea of being

a conventional missionary clergyman. He also met Gandhi. It was love at first sight.

In the biography of C. F. Andrews by Hugh Tinker, there are at the beginning three quotations. The first from Charlie Andrews himself says, "It is no calculating love that will ever win the heart of the East." The other two are from the two men to whom in a remarkable degree he gave that uncalculating love. Gandhi said, "It was love at first sight when I saw him first. . . . If we really love Andrews' memory we may not have hate in us for Englishmen." The statement says a great deal about both of them. The third is from Rabindranath Tagore, who said, "Your love has opened the door of our heart. Enter and welcome, Friend."

These two men opened doors of perception for Andrews – he became a disciple. In the eyes of many of his missionary friends he had abandoned not only his priesthood but his Christian faith. In fact what Gandhi gave him was a new and deeper way of looking at and being identified with Christ, of seeing that the way of renunciation which was so truly the very mark of the life of Christ was possible for him: and not only that. In India Andrews recognised the Christ who draws everyone to himself, regardless of colour, race, class, creed or caste. He saw the injustice of the system, and the condemnation of Christ of those who condemned their fellow human beings to unending poverty.

Inevitably his Christian faith, as it deepened, became identified also with the political necessity of the time. It made him unpopular, but it also attracted others who were longing to present the Christian faith to India in ways which Indian people would understand from their own history, culture, and social and political struggles. Among them were a group of men who looked to C. F. Andrews as a guru – and beyond him to Gandhi himself. Cambridge and Oxford once again played a prominent part. The first of these was John Copley Winslow, known universally as Jack, very much Eton and Balliol – who was at school when

Queen Victoria was celebrated as the Empress of India and Lord Curzon was her Viceroy.

Jack Winslow met C. F. Andrews when he was teaching at St Stephen's College, Delhi, and recognised a kindred spirit. Winslow worked in India – first in high school at Ahmadnaga, and later in Poona, as it was then called. His association with Charlie Andrews developed in a deeply personal and spiritual way. Learning from him, and from others, notably Sahdu Sundar Singh, Winslow finally established an ashram in Poona, built architecturally on Indian lines, with low buildings surrounding a pool, a Christian church which looked like a Hindu temple. There he drew a wide variety of men and women, remarkably, and for those who know India, almost miraculously, High and Low caste, Brahmin, Moslem, Hindu, from far and wide, into a community which in various ways and varying degrees were drawn to Christ. It was called *Christa Seva Sangha (The Society of the Servants of Christ).* That was in 1920. They all wore Indian homespun cotton with a saffron cord, the colour of renunciation. Gandhi spoke with admiration of it – Tagore and Jack exchanged poetry; Andrews remained Jack's spiritual guide.

Winslow came to England a few years later. With his fine mind, his spiritual insight and his zeal for India seen through Indian eyes, he recruited a number of priests and laymen, mostly from the two Universities, who eventually joined him at the ashram. For a while it became a remarkable and visionary place of prayer and learning, and true asceticism. Among them two in particular were outstanding. Verrier Elwin, who left the ashram, became a travelling holy man – and finally left behind his priesthood and his Christian faith. A brilliant anthropologist, he became the Adviser for Tribal Affairs to Pandit Nehru. I nearly met him once in Shillong, Assam – but my well laid plans somehow did not come off, to my great sorrow. In a charmingly Indian fashion it was thought by a bishop that it would be unsuitable for me to meet him – so it just did not happen. It was Verrier Elwin who, with Jack Winslow, wrote the Rule by which the Life of the Ashram was to be lived. It sees the pattern of life very much as one of service, of the acknowledgement of Jesus as our true Master, of the reverence we should have for one another and all creation, "calling nothing common, or unclean", to quote it.

The other outstanding person was William Strowar Amhurst Robertson, who from his time at Cambridge had always been called "Algy". Algy was obliged to return to England with ruined health. He became the Vicar of St Ives, near Cambridge, turned his Vicarage into a branch house of the ashram and began recruiting men who would eventually go out to the ashram in India. He brought with him *The Principles*, the Rule written by Jack and Verrier.

When Algy joined his group of brothers with another small group in Dorset, led by Douglas Down, they formed what is now known as the Society of Saint Francis in the Church of England, and of which I am a member. He also brought with him those same *Principles* – and it is still our Rule of Life – a Rule deeply embedded in the life and spirituality of India written by men who were inspired by the now legendary figure of C. F. Andrews, who in his turn honoured and loved Mahatma Gandhi – and learned from him another way of love. I was Algy's secretary for a number of years: and on the day of Gandhi's death, he declared a day of mourning for all his brothers. The vision of Winslow came to an end – and I was the last brother to stay in the ashram together with Bishop Lash, another of Jack's recruits, who was the last Asharia; but the ashram is still a reality in the care of others, and the vision lives in *The Principles* which is part of our daily life here, and throughout the world. I have heard it read in the depths of New Guinea, in the Solomon Islands, in the heart of Africa, Australia, America: a testimony among other things to those remarkable men, who for want of a better word I would call saints.

Michael Ramsey

A MEMORIAL SERMON

Those whom he predestined he also called:
and those whom he called he also justified:
and those whom he justified he also
glorified.   *Romans 8:30*

In St Bene't's Church, Cambridge. May 1988

ABOUT forty years ago a rather importunate under-graduate in Oxford persuaded me one Sunday to hear the University Sermon because, he said, it was being preached by the greatest priest in the Church of England, and a canon of Durham, from where he came. The young man was right – he is, incidentally, now himself canon of Chichester – the preacher was the Van Mildart Professor in Durham University, Michael Ramsey. I don't remember the sermon, but I vividly remember that first distant encounter with the man.

It was clear that what he had to say he also believed, but more than that, it seemed a part of him. I knew why my friend had wanted me to hear him – I fell, ever so slightly, under a spell.

I met him for the first time about a year later. Together with Father Denis and a dozen undergraduates we had been performing the *Little Plays of St Francis* in various parts of Northumberland and the Borders. Our final performance was in Durham Cathedral and he had offered to put us all up for the night.

After a week of sleeping rough we were a scruffy lot but he seemed to regard it as a great lark. Going up the stairs I encountered a charming girl coming down who said, "I hope you will all be comfortable." I replied, "It's terribly kind of your father to put us all up." She just smiled. When I told another of the party he replied, "You idiot, that's his wife!" He always looked – and acted – like an old man. He also talked like one who had already acquired the wisdom of age – it was for younger men and women a source of deep reassurance. What then were the qualities which in so striking a degree singled him out as unique among the archbishops of this century? The answer comes to us from St Paul this morning.

1. *Those whom he predestined he also called.*

Michael Ramsey was a man called by God. His text at his installation in Canterbury was: "There went with him a band of men whose hearts God had touched."

We are all called by God, all have a destiny, to be the sons and daughters of God, inheritors of the Kingdom of Heaven, rejoicing here and now in eternal life. To that end God calls some to be his ministers, servants of his sons. In Michael Ramsey this was so self-evident, so completely a part of him that it had a radiant power to dispel doubt in others. There was, in some ways, a disarming innocence about him. He knew about sin and about pain, and was a compassionate and loving counsellor. His considerable theological stature was not necessary to his faith, but it became the structure through which, with disarming simplicity, he could make it known to others. Because his heart had been touched by God, it was always in the end the heart of the matter which he gave to others, as heart speaks to heart.

2. *Those whom he called he also justified.*

His lectures here in Cambridge on the Atonement were a revelation to the students who packed into the Divinity School to hear them. In them the work of God in Salvation

126

was brought vividly alive through the constant exploration of this crucial doctrine: "How may man be just before God?" – to be reclaimed from sin, to be at one with God. So he traced the differing views of all the great scholars in the history of the Church as if he knew them as friends – but then in a real sense he did. He was becoming one of them. I know men who treasure those lecture notes, and regret they were never published. And why? Because in the end he was not providing us with information, but allowing the great doctrinal truths of our faith to appeal to our hearts – if it was true for them, then surely, it could be true for us, for me.

3. And those whom he justified he also glorified.

Perhaps it was because he knew himself, through his prayer and simple awareness, the King of Majesty who is also the source of salvation and a loving friend, that for Michael Ramsey the word "Glory" was never far from his lips and always evident in his life.

His outstanding book on the Transfiguration has at the beginning a quotation from *Alice in Wonderland*:

> Humpty Dumpty said, "There's glory for you."
> "I don't know what you mean by 'glory'," said Alice.
> Humpty Dumpty smiled contemptuously, "Of course you don't – till I tell you. I meant 'There's a nice knock down argument for you'."
> "But glory doesn't mean 'a nice knock down argument'," Alice objected.
> "When I use a word," Humpty Dumpty said in rather a scornful tone, "it means just what I choose it to mean, neither more nor less."

Of course once Michael Ramsey had dealt with it, Glory became exactly that, a nice knock down argument – the unanswerable answer to the impossible truths of our faith

– that which our eyes have seen and our hands have handled of the word of life.

"The Word became flesh – and we beheld his glory." The body risen from the tomb, and glory was established as the eternal reality of life. The Ascended Christ goes from Glory to Glory.

And we ourselves can be transfigured into his likeness from Glory to Glory. Michael Ramsey lived this glory – made the possibility of transcendence a reality; through the utter simplicity of his love, his devotion, his powerful prayer, we came to *know* that Glory as the ultimate answer to the doubts, fears and failures of our lives nationally, personally. At a time when Church and Nation are sometimes sorely torn, when strong leadership is identified only with ruthless ideology, his life has been a reminder that the death of Christ meant the life of man, and the glory of the Cross is reflected in the radiant beauty of those whose lives are hid with Christ in God – men whose hearts have been touched – called, redeemed, glorified.

One true glory of his funeral was with the archbishops, bishops, priests, laity who gathered to thank God for him. Who knew also in their hearts that their lives were what they are because he had given a strong lead in holiness.

And so, "From Glory to glory advancing, we praise thee, O Lord."

R.H. Benson

Moses said, "I beg you, show me your
glory."   *Ex. 33:12 – end*

---

*At the service to celebrate the 125th anniversary of
the Society of St John the Evangelist founded in 1866,
in the Community Church, Cowley, Oxford. August 1991*

MANY of us are glad to be here as sons and daughters
of the one great family of Religious in our Church,
and also to express the love and gratitude we owe to your
Father Founder who is, in many ways, the Father of us all.

When families gather to celebrate they invariably settle
down to recalling, yet again, the well rehearsed landmarks
of family history. That is surely no less appropriate today.
But where to begin?

There were no Religious in our Church after the
Reformation, though it remained Catholic as well as
Anglican, even if that Catholicism was sometimes eclipsed.
And then, here in Oxford, God gave the Church three
young men – and they were remarkably young for the rev-
olution they achieved – to fan into flames the dormant
Catholic spirit.

Like the young companions of Daniel, Shadrach,
Meshach and Abednego, they were, as it says there,
"Young men of nobility, at home in all branches of learning,
informed, intelligent and fit for service in the Royal court."
Well, John Keble, John Henry Newman, and Edward
Bouverie Pusey were indeed brilliant scholars and men of
vision who also placed holiness of being above all things,
making them fit indeed for service in the Royal Court of
Heaven. They also believed, from the beginning of the
Oxford Movement, that restoration of the Religious Life

would be no High Church eccentricity but the affirmation of something fundamental to the life and structure of the whole Church, whose corner stone is Christ.

It was a perilous conviction and, like Daniel and his friends, they encountered the flames of conflict and the furnace of antagonism. Their patience and persistence were rewarded.

Let us recall a momentous day in our family history. On Trinity Sunday 1841, Dr Pusey wrote a letter to Newman, the Vicar of the University Church.

> My dear Friend,
> A young lady who is very grateful for your teaching is purposing today to take a vow of holy celibacy. She has difficulties and anxieties in her position. She has attended St Mary's since she has been in Oxford and hopes to receive Holy Communion there today. It was wished that you should know and remember her. You will know her by her being dressed in white with an ivory cross.
> Yours very gratefully and affectionately,
>
> E. B. Pusey

So it was done, quietly, almost secretly. That young lady became the first sister to live the consecrated life of a Religious in our Church since the Reformation. Indeed, Marian Rebecca Hughes became our Sister, yours and mine.

Four years later disaster struck and Newman became a Roman Catholic. Yet the notable event *that* year, 1845, was not, in the end, his departure but a new development in our life, the beginning in London of the first Religious Order for women, dedicated to the Holy Trinity. A triumph indeed.

With Newman gone and Keble living in the country, the challenge in Oxford was taken up by Pusey. Brilliant scholar, man of God, man of prayer, man of sorrow – he was capable of single-minded iron determination. Men and women turned to him as to a rock, and among them a young scholar who gave him unstinted love, loyalty and devotion, shared his scholarship and became his friend. Out of that devotion and trust, that unflinching faith in God, that almost alarming clarity of vision, the Holy Spirit moulded a man to become the founder of the first Religious Order for men in our Church, Richard Meux Benson.

Pusey remained the determined champion of the Religious Life until he died in 1882, nurtured by the nuns at Ascot. In a sense, he even had a hand in later foundations, in that it was in Pusey House, the home of his library, that Charles Gore conceived the Community of the Resurrection, and the first Franciscans formulated their Rule as the Society of the Divine Compassion in 1893.

But the year we commemorate today is 1866. Once again three young men are involved, from Oxford, Cambridge and Harvard. All of them clever, eager-hearted, fit for service in the Royal Court, indeed longing to do so. Benson, now Vicar of Cowley, had been joined by an American, Charles Chapman Grafton, and Samuel Wilberforce O'Neill, and on December 27th, the Feast of St John the Evangelist, these three solemnly vowed their lives to God and became the Society of St John the Evangelist.

To a considerable degree they represented between them the principal characteristics of the Religious Order which emerged. Benson had a worldwide vision and indeed, at the end of his life, was torn between a longing for both America and India. O'Neill's very names, Samuel and Wilberforce, suggest the evangelical fervour of determined missionaries, their belief in the Religious Life itself led them to the regularity of the monastery, but also to becoming confessors for countless convents all over the world. Their scholarship made them teachers and preachers of the faith. They were Catholics yet remained unmistakably Anglican, even English – well, English and American if you like!

But there is more to it than that. Benson's faith places him in the great tradition of the Anglican divines exemplified by Keble, Newman and Pusey, firmly based on the Fathers and the earliest teaching and tradition of the whole Church

These three founders of the first Order for men in our Church shared with them another major characteristic, and one in which they found their strength and tenacity of purpose. It was, put quite simply, the pursuit of holiness, and became a longing in all their lives. It is found in their spiritual instructions, their prayers, addresses and sermons, and not least in those endless lengthy Victorian letters they never tired of writing!

It was this which motivated them and, in Benson's case, led to sleepless nights of prayer alone in that chapel at the top of the Mission house and to his ruthless bodily discipline in his longing to share the holiness of God, to see him in his glory. This world became for him an ante-room of heaven in which he repeatedly echoed the prayer of Moses, "I beg you, show me your glory."

It was this preoccupation with Divinity which gave such power to Benson's love of humanity, the humanity of Christ in man. He longed for the world to be won for Christ. His first love was India, and once he had his bags packed all ready to go. Frustrated himself, he gladly encouraged others and later recognised the sacrifice of Father O'Neill, alone in India, as true to everything he hoped for himself and the Society.

Like other great men and women who founded our Religious Orders he came from the world of affluent middle-class Victorian security. After all, his family were successful brewers – and in fact the family name Meux is still to be found in every pub in the land – only nowadays, through mergers, it is, believe it or not, called *Friary Meux*! He was drawn to poverty not only as a way of reconciling his riches through a personal religious discipline, but

because in the poverty of India Christ could be seen looking at him through the eyes of outcast and sweeper, the
truly poor who have no other choice, as well as Hindus,
Buddhists, Brahmins: he could recognise in them a
supreme motive for the Incarnation of Christ Himself.

And what was true for India became true for America,
Africa, everywhere. Some Cowley fathers are great trav-
ellers, contrary to the expectations of those who only know
them in the confines of the cloister.

I first came to Cowley nearly fifty years ago – having just
joined what was regarded as a rather rough lot of friars
living off the land in deepest Dorset. Cowley, by contrast,
was a bit alarming. The fathers were unfailingly courteous,
but the chapel was intimidating, the recreation formidable,
and even the refectory a bit of a challenge with the same
sense of silence and calm certainty; everyone looked down
– or so it seemed. I once ventured to look up just as a father
was passing, who shot me unexpectedly a smile and then a
large and exaggerated wink! What a relief!

It was Father Manson, and later I went with him on
several parochial missions. Well, times have changed but
those missions were an invaluable introduction to one
aspect of Cowley evangelism.

It was about this time that I also learned of another
Cowley tradition established by Father Benson. I went into
retreat, and to assist me in my meditations was given a
book by a Cowley father closely based on the *Spiritual
Exercises* of Ignatius Loyola. In these days when all roads
lead to St Beuno's it is well to recall that Fr Benson trod that
road long before, and in 1858 took the first retreat for
priests at Cuddesdon, basing his addresses on the *Exercises*,
and in fact had known and admired the Jesuits from the
age of nineteen. More importantly it demonstrates an
aspect of his spirituality that from an early age became an
abiding one and was given by him to his brethren. He said,
"It is the contemplative life, gazing up to God and doing
battle with Satan, that is the essential characteristic of all

Christian life." It certainly was of his in his single-minded and relentless pursuit of holiness.

And finally there was for Fr Benson his belief in the Religious Life itself seen positively, lovingly, courageously. It was a challenge that brought out the fighting spirit in him in the war against Satan.

I was brought up in the novitiate on a book of his into which he poured a great deal of himself and in which you can find, perhaps, something of the heart, even the soul of the man; his commentary on the Psalms with the strikingly paradoxical title *The War Songs of the Prince of Peace*. In the end, he is saying, we are in the world as God's champions, Christ's faithful soldiers and servants engaged in a relentless war against sin, the world and the devil. And that remains as true for us as it was for him.

The most solitary hermit, the most enclosed and silent monk or nun, as well as the endlessly active friars or sisters, know this in their heart. It is no higher calling to be called the shock troops of God: but perhaps we need to recapture some of the enthusiasm and certainty which was there in the first brothers and sisters.

If this present sometimes seems a time of uncertainty, of waiting – well, Fr Benson himself spoke of the enormous value of waiting. We, of all people, should have discovered the "stature of waiting". Waiting seen not as an emptiness between events, but as a true Waiting on God, knowing that "the meaning is in the waiting"; waiting with eager expectation for those who are also waiting to share this life with us.

So as we look forward to the next milestones in our history might we not also cry out with Moses:

I beg you, show me your glory. Put me in the cleft of the rock, let your glory pass by me, and if I only see your back it is enough, for I want to follow you, be led by you into your glory, to see the Vision Glorious.

If this cleft in the rock, the Religious Life, is the way he chose to save you, save me, then it is the only way. We may finally grow in holiness, know his glory, and, sharing in the Victory of the Cross, help to bring the world triumphantly into heaven – singing with joy the "War Songs of the Prince of Peace".

Edward King

A FATHER IN GOD

A paper given to the Bishop King Society,
Ripon College, Cuddesdon. February 1995

WHEN I became a novice in the Society of St Francis over fifty years ago I knew very little about the Religious Life, the Church, or for that matter the Christian faith. Having just left the army in the middle of the war and embarked on that mysterious event in human life and experience we sometimes call conversion – with all its uncertainties and enthusiasms, I knew so little and I had to take a lot on trust. The whole thing had an element of continuous discovery.

One such discovery was that the "High Church" in which I had been confirmed and brought up as a boy (and had deserted at an early age) was part of the same movement as had nurtured the Franciscan Brothers I was hoping to join – the Oxford Movement, or the Tractarians as they were also called. I began to read and get to know its founders and followers, Keble, Newman, and Pusey – to whom I was particularly attracted having been given a collection of his prayers which I found helpful. And then, much more as a person – Bishop King. It was only forty years since his death in 1910, and there were still those who remembered him vividly.

I first heard of him from an old lady, the widow of a priest who had spent most of his ministry in the Diocese of Lincoln. King had been "her" Bishop, and when she spoke of him her whole personality seemed to shine with the memory of his goodness and holiness.

Then, not long after that, as part of our novice training, I was sent regularly to take Evensong in the remote Dorset village of Sydling St Nicholas. The Vicar, a Father Wynne-

Werninck, was ninety and stone deaf! As an undergraduate he had sat at the feet of an ageing Dr Pusey, whom he reverenced; but his love was for Edward King, his ideal of a priest and one on whom he had tried to model himself. Another rather unexpected encounter with him occurred for me in the early biography of King published by B. W. Randolph, at that time Principal of Ely Theological College, and Edward King's chaplain at Lincoln. It tells a story of a student who came to Cuddesdon when King was Principal. Though the young man was the son of a bishop he resented the fact that his Principal had not allowed him to bring his horse, and was determined not to be pushed around by Mr King. He arrived late on a Saturday night: there was a knock on the door and the Principal came in. "Oh, Mr Gray," he said. "I came in to tell you that there is a service in the Church at eight o'clock tomorrow morning, but very likely you will be tired with your journey – so mind you don't get up until after breakfast. It is better not to do so if you are tired." Mr Gray was a young man of iron constitution and resented the idea of being tired. He was there next morning! Charlie Gray became a close friend of Edward King. He also eventually became Vicar of Helmsley in Yorkshire, and a notably holy and caring priest in the Catholic tradition. In 1900 he prepared my mother for Confirmation – and I grew up on the legend of the great C. F. Gray, who was so kind and generous and good to her.

But what really sparked off my enthusiasm for this very human and lovably holy bishop was the discovery of his little book of *Spiritual Letters*, published just after his death, that spoke to me and my condition as if they had all been addressed to me, and have done so ever since. So what made Edward King so unusual, and such an inspiration particularly to those who have been called to be priests?

He was born in 1829, son of an Archdeacon and grandson of a Bishop of Rochester, into the solid comfort of an upper-class Victorian Rectory, one of a family of ten children. Being delicate he was educated at home by his father and the curate to whom he owed his awareness of the Catholic tradition in Anglicanism.

He was devoted to his mother, as she was to him, and indeed she lived with him for the last twenty years of her life.

At the age of eighteen he went up to Oriel College, Oxford, the college which had been identified with several leaders of the Oxford Movement, among them Keble, Pusey, Froude, and most notably John Henry Newman. He had been also Vicar of the University Church. Three years before, in 1845, he had been admitted to the Roman Catholic Church, an event which had rocked the establishment. At Oriel King fell under the spell of two Fellows in particular who, in spite of the prevailing distrust, maintained a Tractarian position; one was Church, who later as Dean Church wrote a notable history of the Oxford Movement, and the other Charles Marriot. Marriot was markedly eccentric, yet carried in him a devotion to Christ which King found compelling. He later called him, "the most Gospel-like man I ever met".

John Newton, in his brief but discerning life of Edward King (*Search for a Saint*) says that "in Marriot, King saw all the great virtues of Tractarianism; its discipline, its holiness, its concern for the poor." He also held in admiration the great scholar of Christ Church, Dr Pusey. With the defection of Newman, and the departure of Keble to a country living, Pusey remained in Oxford defending the Movement, and though constantly criticised, upholding all that he believed to be true of the Catholic position in the Anglican Church.

King was ordained to a curacy at Wheatley, but was not there very long. The bishop, Samuel Wilberforce, who sympathised with the Tractarians, had opened a college at Cuddesdon for training the clergy. Within a few years it had been viciously attacked, partly perhaps because of the uncompromising attitude of its brilliant Vice Principal,

Henry Parry Liddon, who was regarded by opponents as an extreme Romaniser. Into that situation King was appointed as Chaplain, and later, in 1863, he became Principal. It was the beginning of an outstanding ministry of love and care, during which the notable marks of his spiritual life were revealed.

From there, in 1873, he moved into Oxford as a canon of Christ Church, and Regius Professor of Pastoral Theology – a task for which many thought him ill-fitted academically. He was to prove an outstanding example of the pastor and spiritual guide and one who was never to be forgotten for his capacity to change for good the lives of countless students, including young Wynne-Wernink who still recalled him glowing with love and admiration when I met him as a ninety-year-old priest in Dorset.

From there, in 1885, he was appointed Bishop of Lincoln, and at his consecration in St Paul's the same Henry Liddon preached what some regarded as his greatest sermon.

He died in 1910. That is the very bare outline of his life. There were outstanding events during his episcopate, notably his trial on the charge of unlawful Ritualism, which caused him lasting pain, but on the whole he did not play an important part in the national life of the Church. So what made him, and still makes him, so enviably attractive to fellow Christians?

First there was his genuine longing for holiness. There is an old book by Scott-Holland, a younger contemporary of Edward King, called *A Bundle of Memories*. I first heard it read to me in retreat, many years ago. His short memoir of King picks up one fact remarked by many others and that is his sheer attractiveness. He says:

> A light went out of our lives when Edward King passed out of our Companionship. It was light that he carried with him, light that shone through him, light that flowed from him. The room was lit into which he entered.

His holiness and goodness shone out. The testimony is repeated again and again by all sorts of people. No-one who met him ever forgot his face, his eyes, his smile, his natural goodness. It is ironic that he could ever have been thought of as a Romaniser. He was Anglican to his finger-tips, and in the pursuit of holiness takes his place in a spiritual tradition which is both Anglican and English. It is there in the life of Cuthbert and Aelred, in the writings of Richard Rolle and Walter Hilton, the visions of the Lady Julian. And it is also as evident after the Reformation in Jeremy Taylor and George Herbert and Nicholas Ferrar. Charles and John Wesley created the "Holy Club" while they were still students in Oxford, and holiness was the conscious longing of John Keble, and the founders of the Oxford Movement, yet it is also true of Simeon and Henry Martyn. And there are many others up to more recent times.

His ideal of priesthood he learnt from those he admired so much, like Marriot, and by living and learning from others, and it became the mark of his teaching at Cuddesdon. It was a priesthood of the kind of which George Herbert wrote in *The Priest to the Temple*, with a deep love of the sacraments, rooted in the Incarnation and the Passion, owing much to the tradition re-established by Pusey, Liddon and others and given later a wide social reference by Scott-Holland and Gore, and was for him no doctrinaire socialism but a deep identification and profound love for the poor in whom he saw the living Christ. He treated all men and women with the dignity that becomes the living presence of God in them, and with the simplicity that acknowledged with joy their shared humanity.

In common with his contemporaries he could sometimes have a certain reserve – it was notable for instance in Fr Benson the founder of the Cowley Fathers – yet unlike many of them this never obscured his joy and gaiety.

His published sermons, addresses and lectures seem to

lack a little the voice in which they were delivered and must have accounted both for the crowds who came to hear him, and the way in which they were long remembered. But there is one source in which his voice can be heard, and his spirituality acknowledged and that is in the collection of his *Spiritual Letters*.

Edward King was a Victorian, and writing without the inhibitions of our apparently liberated age, could express his love and care in language which would seem in our impoverished times exaggerated or suspect. What his letters reveal is a profound care, a love that sprang from the heart.

The price he paid for it was huge. In one letter, trying to help a young college tutor, he said:

> It will want heaps of talk – mountains of talk – you will have to be worn out and out and done for, and broken hearted and miserable, and not understood, and deceived . . . to bring them all to one heart and soul in earnest, not to yourself, but to the mind of Christ. Then they will love you and you will soon be entangled in helpless love for them. And you will be broken hearted again – and then life will begin.

Another time he wrote, "Anyone who has a high ideal and love of perfection must be prepared to suffer." "Only by breaking your own heart can you hope to make them begin to think of believing that there is such a thing as love." And again, "Don't mind, be miserable, but don't stop loving them."

He was Principal of Cuddesdon when he wrote that. He wrote it about ordinands for ordinands; wrote about himself, his own pain in love; wrote as a past-master in the School of Love, wrote as a friend to friends after the pattern of Aelred of Rievaulx, or Ignatius Loyola – who called his first followers "Friends in the Lord". Wrote above all to teach future priests a pattern of friendship after the example of Jesus – who before he died declared to the apostles, of whom you are the successors, "I have not called you servants, I have called you friends," and died for them and for us.

That was the way it was expressed: but what lay behind it is this particular longing for his own holiness, and the holiness of those for whom he lived, whether in the scholarly world of Cuddesdon and Oxford, or among the plough-boys and shepherds of his great fenland diocese.

Liddon's sermon at his consecration was, prophetically, on the bishop as "A Father in Christ". It is a very long sermon, and gives a masterly perspective to his subject, theologically and historically. Towards the end he begins to wind up. "The title 'Father in God' has never disappeared whether in the language of the Church or the Law . . . the essential features of a spiritual fatherhood remain intact." And continues later speaking of King:

> Never probably in our times has the great grace of sympathy, controlled and directed by a clear sense of the nature and sacredness of revealed truth achieved so much among so many young men as has been achieved at Cuddesdon, and then from the Pastoral Chair at Oxford. He is surrounded at this solemn moment by hundreds who know and feel that to his care and patience, to his skill and courage, to his faith and spiritual insight, they owe all that is most precious in life.

All this, as Father in God to the student world he transferred unreservedly to his diocese, and in love for his priests, their families, and his largely rural and impoverished people. There are endless stories of his natural and unconsciously committed love and friendship for the simple people he met in the villages. They are stories characterised by a capacity to communicate the "otherness" of our faith in a way which is rare. It is remarkable that in the Lincoln diocese he is remembered not only for his holiness, but in particular for his love and understanding of the poor. His loss to Oxford and the academic world was regarded at the time as tragic. The wholeness of his holiness is remarkable only in that as a bishop it was expressed so completely in so different a world, or indeed, in that he was there for twenty-five years, in the minds of many to completely overshadow his earlier ministry. The possibility had not been lost on Liddon, who foresaw an episcopate to be compared with Lancelot Andrewes, Bishop Ken, and others. What might not have been foreseen is that he would quite naturally, and as if it were what his whole ministry was leading to, become the Bishop of the Poor, acknowledging his gladness to be in the diocese of John Wesley, whose pursuit of holiness led him also unreservedly to the poor. King was in the same tradition of Evangelical Catholicism as Wesley and longed for that schism to be repaired, blaming it on the lack of charity and brotherly love of the episcopate of that time.

So the pursuit of holiness led him to recognise holiness in others and in his role as Father in God to respond with his own intensive capacity for human love to the countless men, women and children among whom he moved so tirelessly, unselfconsciously and without condescension.

Newton spoke of the marks of Tractarianism as discipline, holiness and love for the poor. And it is important to note the significant place played by discipline in the High Church tradition of Evangelical Catholicism.

Though Newman and others left for Rome, those who remained affirmed even more certainly the essential Catholicity of the Anglican Church, in its devotion to the Bible, the Book of Common Prayer, the psalms, sacraments and episcopal ministry. Their determination to reclaim and reassert the regular praying of the Daily Office, use of the litanies and observance of the days of fasting, and the centrality of the Eucharist led to a disciplined life of prayer which was the foundation of their spiritual life. There were many battles with those who feared the influence of Rome, because of course it also led to the restoration and decoration of the churches as an aid to worship, the appearance of candles, and, with a heightened awareness of sin, that which was feared most of all, the "popish" practice of auricular confession and the rising power of priests, with their vestments, superstitions, and all the rest.

There is a story often repeated of the shepherd to whom King explained why candles were alight on the altar, even though it was broad daylight, and who replied, "Oh, I see, Sir, yours is a yon-side religion." In a very real sense he always had the capacity of bringing the "yon-side" into the present, and used candles only to that end, as he brought the forgiveness of God into the present in the Confessional.

It was as a consequence tragic that he was so publicly put on trial as a ritualist, and sanctified by suffering.

The earliest Tractarians were little interested in outward ritual, but the Church Association, an organisation always on the look-out for signs of popery, had their eye on King from the time he became bishop. He was indeed the first bishop to wear a mitre since the Reformation, but by most standards the accusations made against him would seem to us very modest indeed. Taking the eastward position; having lighted candles on the altar, blessing with the sign of the cross, mixing water with the wine, and so on.

The trial was notable, in part because it asserted the jurisdiction by right of the Archbishop, and Archbishop Benson seems to have taken full advantage of it, presiding in state in the library at Lambeth over a special court, assisted by six diocesan bishops. The trial was a lengthy proceeding, and judgement was not finally delivered until many months later. It opened on February 12th and judgement was given on November 21st, substantially in King's favour. In the meantime petitions were signed, funds raised, and Edward King was widely praised and supported.

But it took its toll on him. Never robust, it was noted how strained and stooped he became, though the peace and patient love never left him. It was thought by some that he never recovered entirely.

The fashion for defining spirituality too closely with particular peoples, attitudes or traditions is a little unreal. I would certainly find it difficult to say there was, or is, a spirituality of Edward King, beyond that which he holds in common with some other outstanding holy men and women in our Church. There is, as has been said, (and the point has been made by several of those who have written about him) something particularly Anglican and English about him. A certain understatement, a sense of very natural holiness, a very courteous, almost gentlemanly concern for others. And yet a disarming open-heartedness towards God and mankind of a very personal and human kind which, because there are no barriers, no restraints, no false modesty, shyness or artificial diffidence, allows the full blaze of God's glory to flood through. It is something we catch in the metaphysical poets from Henry Vaughan and Traherne all the way to Gerard Manley Hopkins.

This very personal and human understanding of Divinity is something we find again and again in our history, bursting out with great vigour in the hymns of Charles Wesley, no less than in the more moderate verse of Keble's *Christian Year.*

It happens that at about the same time as I came upon the *Spiritual Letters* of Edward King I also found a new edition of another great spiritual classic, Aelred's treatise *On Christian Friendship,* and indeed they rubbed shoulders on my bookshelf. Aelred was Abbot of Rievaulx in the twelfth century and promoted an astonishing growth of the Cistercian life there. I think there would have been an instant point of recognition between them. Both speak with uninhibited love of all that friendship with God meant to them, as it captured their whole lives: and both spoke with the same uninhibited love that they had for all the people they believed God had led to them in the same bond of friendship.

The monks of Rievaulx looked back with great wonder to the days when Aelred was Abbot, and no less the priests and former scholars at Cuddesdon and Oxford, as well as the greatest and the most humble of the people of Lincolnshire, looked back with love and wonder to the days when King was their Father in Christ. In both was that quality of life which for want of a better word we call holiness, and settle for saying they are saints.

Charles Wesley

REFLECTIONS ON THE PASSION IN THE HYMNS OF CHARLES WESLEY

St Bene't's Church, Cambridge. February 1995

CHARLES Wesley is sometimes regarded as "brother of the more famous John", a misleading and erroneous judgement. John Wesley is undoubtedly a towering figure in the history of the Church in this land and the founding father of a religious movement which numbered hundreds of thousands in his own lifetime. Methodism now has perhaps twenty million followers world wide; yet it can be questioned whether that growth would have been possible without Charles. If John was the mind of the movement Charles, through his hymns, expressed its heart. Though it eventually attracted men and women of substance it was, in the first place, a movement which spoke to the needs of the common people, coalminers in Bristol, industrial workers in Newcastle, tin miners in Cornwall, and agricultural labourers everywhere. The desperately poor and illiterate came to hear John in their thousands – and expressed their response in the hymns of Charles, learning them by heart and singing them to popular tunes. It is a tradition which exists to this day. To hear the mighty roar of a Welsh chapel singing the hymns of Wesley to Welsh tunes is a particular and characteristic mark of the whole movement. To understand the significance of this may I first remind you briefly of how it all came to be – though it can only be a very bare outline.

Charles Wesley was the youngest son of the Revd Samuel and Susannah Wesley, the Rector of Epworth in Lincolnshire. He was born in 1707 and had two older brothers, John and Samuel, and thirteen sisters (it sounds a lot, but Susannah's mother had twenty-four children – it was not so unusual in those days!).

His father was remarkable, clever and very eccentric, much given to writing epic poetry. He was a high Churchman and often at war with the dissenters in his parish. Susannah was a tower of strength managing to organise her family against a background of poverty, and, frequently, debt. She too was something of a scholar, a woman of courage and tenacity, who undertook the education of the boys until they went to school. From the age of five every child studied for six hours a day – and all became proficient in Latin and Greek. They also took a full part in the prayer life of the family and the study of scripture, learning a great deal of the New Testament by heart.

It is notable in the hymns of Charles how every line echoes his wide knowledge of the whole Bible. Of the 7,400 hymns attributed to him over 5,000 consist of a commentary on verses systematically drawn from the whole Bible.

John went to Charterhouse School, Samuel and Charles to Westminster School in London, and from there all three passed on to Christ Church, Oxford. John, pre-eminently the greater scholar, later became a Fellow of Lincoln College, Oxford. Later still all three became priests. All their lives they affirmed their membership of the Church of England, in which they were baptised and ordained, and more than that they never forsook that High Church tradition, focused on the sacraments and adherence to the Book of Common Prayer in which they had been brought up at Epworth. That in itself singled them out at Oxford. But more than that they also began to challenge the mood of laxity and indifference to the faith and practice which prevailed not only there but in the Church at large throughout the country. This was the century of the Georges, indeed the Church had drifted into sloth and corruption from the time of Queen Anne. Outside the Church were numerous sects characterised by hostility to an established church which, from the time of the Act of Uniformity in 1662, had insisted on the acceptance of episcopal ordination to the ministry, and adherence to the Book of Common Prayer absolutely. On top of that the Toleration Act of 1689 had given non-conformists the right to meet together for worship in their own chapels. In general the nonconformists were defined as dissenters.

In Charles and his brother there grew a real longing for holiness. Charles in his search for this invited a few friends and fellow students to join him for prayer, the study of scripture, and regular attendance at Holy Communion. The group was sometimes derisively mocked as "The Holy Club". Among them was George Whitefield, who was later to become a notable evangelist. They were serious about their study, serious about their spiritual life, and together drew up a rule of conduct. Getting up very early for prayer, meeting each evening from six to nine for intercession, attending Communion every Sunday (at a time when three times a year was more the custom), observing Wednesdays and Fridays as fast days – and later visiting the poor and prisoners. This was their Method and Charles was the first to be called a "Methodist".

With hostility from outside and growing enthusiasm inside, Charles called on John to come and help these "Methodists", and he, with all his thoroughness and organising skill became the inspired leader of "The Holy Club".

Soon after leaving Oxford they responded to the challenge of a General Oglethorpe to go on a perilous journey to America to help him in the establishing of a new colony, to preach the gospel and convert the Indians. It was not an entire success and after sickness and disappointment they returned to England. But they were still determined to preach the revival of faith, and return to the Gospel and the Church. Finding like-minded people who gathered to share in the discovery of Christ in their lives, a group began meeting in Fetter Lane off Fleet Street in London.

Then on May 21st, 1738, at the age of 31, a crucial event took place that was to change and deepen the life of

Charles. He had returned from America to serious illness. In the course of his recovery in the house of a faithful Christian friend he prepared for Pentecost. There he was suddenly overwhelmed with a sense of Assurance, the knowledge in his heart that he was indeed Saved. The awareness of all that meant to him is reflected in the hymn he wrote to celebrate it.

> Where shall my wondering soul begin?
> How shall I all to Heaven aspire?

But the degree to which this was indelibly impressed on his life is even more clearly expressed in those hymns by which his conversion remained the source of inspiration in all his teaching and preaching. Of those the most widely known, and perhaps one of the finest, is based on the story of Jacob wrestling with the angel – with its moving acknowledgement of the power of the Cross. It concludes:

> 'Tis love! 'tis love! Thou diedst for me!
> I hear thy whisper in my heart;
> The morning breaks, the shadows flee,
> Pure, universal Love thou art:
> To me, to all, thy mercies move;
> Thy nature and thy name is Love.

Three days later on the night of May 24th, while John was at a meeting for prayer in London, hearing the reading of a book by Luther on Romans, he too was converted. John said, "I felt my heart strangely warmed, I felt I did trust in Christ, Christ alone for my Salvation." And that remains a notable date in the history of Methodism to this day.

Now the revival was really underway. They began preaching in London churches and John with his organising skill began forming their followers into societies. The Holy Club of the old Oxford days came to their support – notably George Whitefield who outstripped them by the eloquence and power of his preaching. They also began to feel the antagonism of some clergy who refused them their pulpits, were fearful of their doctrine of salvation, and their enthusiasm.

Whitefield, who had moved to Bristol, had the same experience; and defied the bishops by preaching in the open air. He called on John and Charles to help.

Thus began a unique ministry, and an itinerant life, notably for John, who was hardly ever still, and who covered, it is estimated, many thousands of miles on horseback and preached almost to his dying day. And all was supported by an outpouring of hymns by Charles. There has never been seen its like.

There were several collections of hymns made as the years went by and from them a major book was published by John, known as *The Large Hymn Book* – it has been described as "A Methodist Manifesto". The version most widely known appeared in 1780, and was used until 1904.

It is called *A Collection of Hymns for the use of the People called Methodists*. Together with a supplement added later there are 769 hymns – and almost all of them by Charles. It is no haphazard collection as is pointed out firmly by John in the Preface. There he calls it "a full and distinct account of Scriptural Christianity . . . a clear direction for making your calling and direction sure . . . for perfecting holiness in the fear of God."

Bernard Manning, senior tutor of Jesus College, Cambridge, and a lecturer in history in the University, who died in 1942, in a book on the hymns of Charles Wesley and Isaac Watts says of *The Large Book*: "this little book ranks in Christian literature with the Psalms, the Book of Common Prayer, the Canon of the Mass. It is," he says, "a work of supreme devotional art by a religious genius". Well, yes, perhaps, if you allow that even the greatest poets can lapse into doggerel, as he sometimes certainly did.

For me the overriding impression in the hymns is a great sense of celebration. Celebrating the power and glory of God; celebrating Jesus the Incarnate Son and Saviour;

celebrating His intervention in our lives; our conversion
and the transformation that follows; celebrating the degree
to which everything in us, body, mind and spirit are
changed by the saving power of Jesus, and the astonishing
liberty and freedom it gives us. Just think of some of the
great hymns we all know – "Christ, whose glory fills the
skies", "Let saints on earth in concert sing with those
whosework is done", "O, for a thousand tongues to sing
my dear Redeemer's praise". Above all they are hymns
which everywhere recognise and rejoice in the love of God.
And because the offering of His life on the Cross is central
to that salvation, so the Cross, and the new life in the Spirit,
is a recurring theme. For the purpose of this talk I must
limit myself to three points of reference in his   experience
which he seeks to express and share in his hymns. Needless
to say it would be possible to define others.

Firstly there is his conversion; secondly, that activity
which was central to his ministry and his brother, the work
of evangelism and preaching the Gospel; and thirdly that
which was central to his spirituality, the Holy Communion
service; and all these reflecting the glory of God and His
love.

We have already noted the hymns which were a direct
result of his conversion, notably the concluding verse of
"Struggling Jacob". The version in *The Large Hymn Book* has
twelve verses.

You will remember the story. Jacob is alone, all his family and flock have gone ahead. All night long there is a fierce
conflict in him, as he struggles with God, who asks him his
name but Jacob replies by demanding in return the name of
God. Wesley says in verses omitted in most contemporary
books:

> In vain thou strugglest to get free,
> I never will unloose my hold!
> Art thou the Man that died for me?
> The secret of thy love unfold:

Wrestling, I will not let thee go,
Till I thy Name, thy Nature know.

Wilt thou not yet to me reveal
Thy new, unutterable Name?
Tell me, I still beseech thee, tell:
To know it now, resolved I am:
Wrestling, I will not let thee go,
Till I thy Name, thy Nature know.

What though my shrinking flesh complain,
And murmur to contend so long?
I rise superior to my pain:
When I am weak, then I am strong!
And when my all of strength shall fail,
I shall with the God-Man prevail.

My prayer hath power with God: the grace
Unspeakable I now receive;
Through faith I see thee face to face:
I see thee face to face, and live!
In vain I have not wept and strove;
Thy Nature and thy Name is Love.

I know thee, Saviour, who thou art,
Jesus, the feeble sinner's Friend:
Nor wilt thou with the night depart,
But stay and love me to the end;
Thy mercies never shall remove;
Thy nature and thy name is Love.

So he asks the great question, "Art thou the Man that died
for me?" There is a faint echo of Galatians 2:20 "who loved
me, and who gave himself for me", a text on which John
Wesley preached almost more often than any other. But he
persists.

Wrestling I will not let thee go
Till I Thy name, thy Nature know.

Later the fulfilment, the overwhelming grace of God leads
Jacob to the knowledge of his name:

> 'Tis love! 'tis love! thou diedst for me!
> I hear thy whisper in my heart:
> The morning breaks, the shadows flee,
> Pure, universal Love thou art:
> To me, to all, thy mercies move;
> Thy nature and thy name is Love.

A further development of his devotion to the saving
power of Jesus is in a hymn to be used at the New Year,
a time when Methodists renew their Solemn Covenant
with God – and makes the point of Jesus our Advocate. It
concludes:

> Today while it is called today
> The hindering thing remove;
> And, lo, I now begin to pray
> And wrestle for thy love.

> I now from all my sins would turn
> To my atoning God;
> And look on Him I pierced, and mourn,
> And feel the sprinkled blood:
> Would nail my passions to the cross,
> where my Redeemer died;
> And all things count but dung and loss,
> For Jesus crucified.

> Giver of penitential pain,
> Before thy cross I lie,
> In grief determined to remain,
> Till thou thy blood apply.
> Forgiveness on my conscience seal,
> Bestow thy promised rest;
> With purest love thy servant fill,
> And number with the blest.

Notice that it picks up the thought of wrestling with God. Notice also the emphasis on the blood of Jesus, which occurs frequently. We are reminded that the blood of Jesus is His life – the life He gave for us on the Cross.

Let me return to a hymn which draws together all the elements in the fulfilment of saving grace, and illustrates the Doctrine of salvation as he understood it – but also reflects the love and joy which was always present for him as he dwelt on it.

> O God of our forefathers, hear,
> And make thy faithful mercies known
> To thee, through Jesus, we draw near,
> Thy suffering well-beloved Son,
> In whom thy smiling face we see,
> In whom thou art well-pleased with me.
>
> With solemn faith we offer up,
> And spread before thy glorious eyes,
> That only ground of all our hope,
> That precious, bleeding Sacrifice,
> Which brings thy grace on sinners down,
> And perfects all our souls in one.
>
> Acceptance through his only name,
> Forgiveness in his blood, we have;
> But more abundant life we claim
> Through him, who died our souls to save
> To sanctify us by his blood,
> And fill with all the life of God.
>
> Father, behold thy dying Son,
> And hear the blood that speaks above!
> On us let all thy grace be shown:
> Peace, righteousness, and joy, and love,
> Thy kingdom, – come to every heart,
> And all thou hast, and all thou art.

Another hymn which was of particular importance to

Charles, summing up for him all his devotion to the atoning work of Jesus, begins:

> All ye that pass by,
> To Jesus draw nigh:
> To you is it nothing that Jesus should die?
> Your ransom and peace,
> Your surety he is;
> Come, see if there ever was sorrow like his.

And after reminding us that Jesus prayed for our forgiveness concludes:

> His death is my plea;
> My advocate see,
> And hear the blood speak that hath answer'd
> for me:
> Acquitted I was
> When he bled on the cross;
> And by losing his life he hath carried my cause.

  Indeed some of his hymns read like a sustained meditation on the Passion such as this, containing perhaps more vivid imagery than would seem appropriate to some people:

> Extended on a cursed tree
> Besmear'd with dust, and sweat, and blood
> See there, the King of Glory see!
> Sinks and expires the Son of God!
>
> Who, who, my Saviour, this hath done?
> Who could thy sacred body wound?
> No guilt thy spotless heart hath known,
> No guile hath in thy lips been found.
>
> I, I alone, have done the deed!
> 'Tis I thy sacred flesh have torn;
> My sins have caused thee, Lord, to bleed,
> Pointed the nail, and fix'd the thorn.

The burden, for me to sustain
Too great, on thee, my Lord, was laid;
O heal me, thou hast born my pain;
To bless me, thou a curse wast made.

My Saviour, how shall I proclaim,
How pay, the mighty debt I owe?
Let all I have, and all I am,
Ceaseless to all thy glory show.

Too much to thee I cannot give;
Too much I cannot do for thee;
Let all thy love, and all thy grief,
Graven on my heart for ever be!

The meek, the still, the lowly mind,
O may I learn from thee, my God;
And love, with softest pity join'd,
For those that trample on thy blood!

Still thy tears, thy groans, thy sighs,
O'erflow my eyes, and heave my breast,
Till loose from flesh and earth I rise,
And ever in thy bosom rest.

or this:

Ye that pass by, behold the Man,
The Man of Griefs, condemn'd for you!
The Lamb of God, for sinners slain,
Weeping to Calvary pursue.
See! how his back the scourges tear,
While to the bloody pillar bound!

So he preached what he knew from his personal experience.

And now we turn to the Eucharist, which was of absolute importance in his own personal spiritual life. The same truth was demonstrated for him by the mighty act of God in Christ which had given us the memorial of his love in the Eucharist, and some of his finest hymns. Regular and frequent attendance at the Lord's table had been a mark of the Holy Club, and remained central in the teaching of John and Charles. It was indeed because his people were excluded from the churches and the sacraments that John was driven finally to ordain some of his preachers and particularly Dr Thomas Coke as effectively a bishop, an act which Charles roundly condemned. He wrote:

> So easily are Bishops made
> By man or woman's whim,
> Wesley his hand on Coke has laid
> But who laid hands on him?

For John (as for Charles) the Eucharist was a memorial of that sacrifice by which we are saved from sin, so the sacrament took precedence for him even over preaching. He said, "I found much of the Power of God in preaching, but far more at the Lord's Table."

For me one of the finest of his hymns, appearing in many collections (usually deplorably truncated, and not very often sung) begins "Victim Divine thy grace we claim".

> Victim Divine, thy grace we claim,
> While thus thy precious death we show:
> Once offer'd up, a spotless Lamb,
> In thy great temple here below,
> Thou didst for all mankind atone,
> And standest now before the throne.
>
> Thou standest in the holy place,
> As now for guilty sinners slain;
> The blood of sprinkling speaks, and prays,
> All prevalent for helpless man;
> Thy blood is still our ransom found,
> And speaks salvation all around.
>
> The smoke of thy atonement here
> Darken'd the sun, and rent the veil,

Made the new way to heaven appear,
And show'd the great Invisible:
Well pleased in thee, our God look'd down,
And calls his rebels to a crown.

He still respects thy Sacrifice;
Its savour sweet doth always please;
The Offering smokes through earth and skies,
Diffusing life, and joy, and peace:
To these, thy lower courts, it comes,
And fills them with divine perfumes.

We need not now go up to heaven,
To bring the long-sought Saviour down;
Thou art to all already given,
Thou dost even now thy banquet crown:
To every faithful soul appear,
And show thy real presence here!

So he picks up the doctrine of the atonement as sacrifice; Jesus the Spotless Lamb, both Victim and High Priest, who stands before the throne of God, pleading for us, with whom He identified himself; his Heavenly banquet is realised on earth, and we know His Real Presence with us. And in all this he acknowledges the power of the Holy Spirit – as in another short hymn:

Come, Holy Ghost, thine influence shed,
And realize the sign;
Thy life infuse into the bread,
Thy power into the wine.

Effectual let the tokens prove,
And made, by heavenly art,
Fit channels to convey thy love
To every faithful heart.

He reminds us too of the grace and power of the sacramental bread and wine:

159

The grace which sure salvation brings
Let us herewith receive;
Satiate the hungry with good things,
The hidden manna give.

The living bread, sent down from heaven,
In us vouchsafe to be:
Thy flesh for all the world is given,
And all may live by thee.

Now, Lord, on us thy flesh bestow,
And let us drink thy blood,
Till all our souls are fill'd below
With all the life of God.

This is only a slight taste of the riches to be found in the
hymns of Charles Wesley – a man who in his own lifetime
was "changed" "from glory into glory", and surely shares
now the joy of heaven which he proclaimed so clearly on
earth. I would like to conclude with a hymn in which
Charles Wesley expresses all the longing of his own heart.
He sees the Cross as a foretaste of heaven, embracing the
bold idea of "Jesus our Crucified God". It is a hymn in
which we hear, in the most intimate and personal terms, all
that the Passion of Jesus meant to him:

Thou Shepherd of Israel, and mine,
The joy and desire of my heart;
For closer communion I pine,
I long to reside where thou art:
The pasture I languish to find,
Where all, who their Shepherd obey,
Are fed, on thy bosom reclined,
And screen'd from the heat of the day.

Ah! show me that happiest place,
The place of thy people's abode,
Where saints in an ecstasy gaze,
And hang on a crucified God:

Thy love for a sinner declare,
Thy passion and death on the tree;
My spirit to Calvary bear,
To suffer and triumph with thee.

'Tis there, with the lambs of thy flock,
There only, I covet to rest,
To lie at the foot of the rock,
Or rise to be hid in thy breast:
'Tis there I would always abide,
And never a moment depart;
Conceal'd in the cleft of thy side,
Eternally held in thy heart.

St Francis of Assisi

THE SPIRITUALITY OF ST FRANCIS

Ridley Hall, Cambridge. January 1994

I AM a little wary about seeking to define a pattern of spirituality derived from the life and writings of St Francis; the tradition established by the Orders which sprang from his original foundation; or the formidable literature available concerning him, from his lifetime to the present day. Francis is remarkably well documented and the official lives of Thomas of Celano written very soon after his death and followed a few years later by the even more official life of St Bonaventure (which corrected Celano in certain respects) are surrounded by the other contemporary writings on which has been built through the ages a thriving industry of Franciscan studies.

The little poor man of Assisi for all his simplicity has so many facets to his character that he is, with some justification, claimed as the supreme exemplar for countless causes. This glorious and unparalleled diamond reflects the purest light from a thousand sharply defined faces in all the iridescent colours of the rainbow. His appeal is nothing if not contemporary. His love of creation, and his care for creatures, makes him the clearest candidate as patron saint of the Green Party and advocate for the environmentalists; his love of peace and reconciliation suggest that San Francisco was the logical place for the United Nations Charter to be signed; and when, some years ago, the Pope invited the leaders of all the religions of the world to join with him to fast and pray for peace, it was natural that they met in Assisi. One of his most recent and distinguished biographers, Leonardo Boff, the Latin American theologian, has identified him, quite rightly, with liberation

162

theology, and the option for the poor. It may be remembered that even Margaret Thatcher tried to quote him on the steps of No 10 when she took over as Prime Minister, though I must confess a monetarist policy, privatisation and the dominance of market forces of the kind we have experienced in the past years hardly lived up to that promise.

It was pointed out by John Moorman, the distinguished Anglican Franciscan scholar, that we can all too easily make the mistake of confusing Franciscan spirituality with the spirituality of St Francis – an elusive thing if it exists at all. So how might we arrive at a spirituality that could properly be called Franciscan?

Early life and conversion

Francis was born in 1182, the son of a wealthy merchant Pietro Bernardone. It was not his baptismal name, but one conferred on him by his father. He died in Assisi forty-four years later in 1226.

Assisi is a small walled city on a hill overlooking an Umbrian plain. It is singularly beautiful and well preserved – indeed nowadays almost too well preserved – no doubt saved down the ages because of the saintly son who is buried there. Except that the castle on its peak is a ruin it would probably be easy for Francis to recognise it today even if its streets are a little sanitised for the sake of the tourists. He would certainly be astonished by the vast number of coaches that come thundering along to disgorge the many thousands of visitors who make for the one great feature that was not there in his day – the huge basilica and monastery, a masterpiece of mediaeval architecture and engineering, including three churches one on top of the other. He is buried in the lowest and simplest, the rest are covered with some of the greatest painting in Italy, indeed in Europe, by Giotto, Cimabue, Lorenzetti, Simone Martine

163

and others – all a tribute to this little man who died naked on the bare earth.

He lived against a background of war. On the world stage of his day there were the Crusades; on the national scale, challenges made to the Emperor; and more locally there were constant feuds between the small cities, notably between Assisi and Perugia. Even within the cities they could be quick to arms. Francis was attracted by the idea of knighthood and chivalry.

He was born into a thriving, wealthy merchant class. For twenty years Francis lived the carefree life of the favourite son of a rich father, a sort of 12th century "yuppie". According to the chronicles, the wealthy young charmer who enjoyed dressing up was the accepted leader of the young men of Assisi.

Francis was also a romantic. He delighted in the ideas of romantic love and the songs of the wandering scholars and troubadours – was indeed a singer himself. All these, chivalry, commerce, romance, had in different ways a profound effect on him.

He was not particularly sinful or wicked, and there are suggestions that he had a care for those less fortunate than himself.

Then in 1204, at the age of twenty-two, there began a series of events, divine initiatives, to which he made a response and which led cumulatively to his conversion and a radical change in his life. These must be mentioned because they are the essential scaffolding around which his whole spiritual life was built.

1. The first occurred because Francis longed to be a knight and fight in a heroic war; and the opportunity was offered for him to go off to fight in a war in Apulia. So, resplendently and colourfully robed in knightly armour, he set off. The first stop on the journey to the war was at Spoleto, and there he had a disturbing dream in which God clearly spoke to him and told him to return to Assisi and await further instructions. "Which is better," said Our

Lord, "to serve the Master or the servant?" This surely was an appalling thing to ask. To turn back, confront all those who had seen him off, be branded as a coward, have no very convincing story to account for it. But it was so powerful a message that he went. It was not the first time he had gone to fight. Once before he had joined in a skirmish in Perugia and ended up in prison. In these experiences lay perhaps his later devotion to peace – the word most frequently on his lips, the greeting he invariably used and encouraged others to use. For the seeds of uncertainty had been sown – and a discontent with his life. Though he took up his carefree life again, he could be moody – once in the middle of some revels he became struck in a sort of trance, and it was assumed by his friends he must be in love. His reply only confused them and himself – he was in love with a lady more beautiful than any earthly bride – the Lady Poverty.

2. The second event took place in a small broken-down church outside Assisi, further down towards the plain. Bare and deserted it had only a large crudely painted crucifix – and he went there to pray; waiting for the answer. When it came he heard himself being told, "Francis, go and build my church which you see is in ruins." And that led to the third episode.

3. Francis returned to Assisi and immediately began to collect material to rebuild the little church, bewildering his friends and frightening his mother – making his father angry, not least because he sold some of his father's cloth to buy stones. It came finally to breaking point. His father tried locking him up, but it didn't work. He was taken to the Bishop where his father demanded justice. In front of the Bishop and his father, and no doubt many others who had come to see what would happen, Francis spontaneously stripped himself naked and said, "From henceforth I will know only one Father, my Father in Heaven." The Bishop hastily covered him with his own cloak until something could be brought to put on him and then,

wearing only a rough shepherd's tunic, he left them all and strode away singing! To begin with he lived rough – a vagrant life, and this led to an encounter, which made an even more profound impression on him.

4. Francis met a leper. Lepers were no unusual sight in thirteenth century Italy: they were outcasts, and lived in leprosariums outside the town. They were regarded as contagious, and as good as dead. It is clear that Francis was horrified by lepers, and had always avoided them. On this occasion, meeting one on a lonely road he was prompted by God to overcome his loathing, embrace him, kiss him, and return with him to the leper colony. And that is where he began his new life, looking after lepers, living as one of them, in Gubbio. But he had to return, and later that year, 1206, came back to Assisi, continued his building work at San Damiano, and began wearing the habit of a hermit. Which defines the fifth episode in his conversion – and the one about which we know least – though it is almost certainly the most important if we are to accept the spiritual awakening of Francis.

5. Francis became a hermit. In this respect Francis followed the same pattern as Benedict and other saints who have been driven to a place of loneliness – or aloneness with God. Subiaco for instance (I mean, of course, the original cave in which Benedict lived) is very much like the lonely places which were loved by Francis. At any rate, for two years or more Francis more or less disappears from sight. Thomas of Celano calls it "the years of conversion". I am sure myself that it is the real key to all that follows – and our own starting point for a way of following Jesus and growing in the Spiritual life after the example of Francis.

The way of prayer

We are fortunate in having a number of writings that can with confidence be attributed to Francis himself. Among these, and possibly the most important, is *The Testament*, which is almost a "Last Will and Testament", written not long before he died. He begins by confessing the degree to which, before his conversion, he feared and detested lepers.

> When I was in sin the sight of lepers nauseated me beyond measure. But then God led me into their company and I had pity on them. What had previously nauseated me became a source of spiritual consolation. After that I did not wait long before leaving the world.

So he left the world to live in caves.

These hidden years are essential to an understanding of Francis. Though the rest of his life was one of endless arduous activity, travel, pain, preaching, with a huge Order growing up all round him, a life dominated by the desire to communicate Jesus to others, all flowed from that deep sense of union with Christ which sprang from his own contemplation. At the beginning it was in the silence, alone with Christ, that he heard Him before the Crucifix in San Damiano, and near the end of his life he was to be united with him again in His Passion. Indeed there came a point some years later when he was so torn with the longing to spend all his life in contemplation that he felt constrained to consult two or three of those who were closest to him and ask their advice. It was a time when his leadership was very much needed and their advice to carry on with his ministry was possibly governed by that need. But there is no doubt where his own longing would have taken him.

Among his writings there is a short but touching and very human *Letter to Hermits* – which makes it clear that he encouraged others to do what he himself was denied, and certainly all over Italy there are the remains (sometimes *too* well restored) of the little hermitages.

To suppose that a spiritual life inspired by the life of Francis should therefore only be associated with a very active apostolate is rather misleading.

Two years later Francis received what he saw as another sign from God when he heard the Gospel read, in which Jesus sent out his disciples to preach, two by two. So he changed his habit as a hermit for a simple one made by himself to resemble a cross, and with a rope round his waist and bare feet, set out to preach, still living in small deserted churches. His example was such that others came to join him and in the spring of 1209 he took his first eleven disciples with him to Rome and secured the Pope's permission to be a Religious Order based on a simple rule – largely texts of scripture. A year later a young girl from Assisi came to join him and she, together with other women who came later, including her sister, were installed in the small church Francis had restored, San Damiano, becoming the foundation of an Order of Sisters known as Franciscans as the Second Order, devoted entirely to a strictly enclosed life of poverty, prayer and contemplation.

It was a place particularly dear to Francis, representing the life he longed for himself.

But it was not to be. He was short, not particularly handsome, and had no special gifts. Certainly he was no organiser. Yet the compelling power of his presence, his commitment to Christ and his totally self–forgetting, sacrificial love proved a magnet to men. By 1221, only twelve years later, when a Chapter meeting was held by the little church he had restored and made his headquarters at St Mary of the Angels, not far from Assisi, it is said that there were five thousand friars – all present, living in the open or under rough huts hastily put together from branches of trees. They came from all classes and backgrounds, noblemen, scholars, priests, simple countrymen, from all over Europe. What drew them? Put rather simply it was this one little man who in his integrity and total surrender to Christ revealed a spiritual path of love. A profound love for creatures, for man and for God.

His love for Creation

Poverty for Francis became a radical concept, and, as in all he said and did, an affirmation of truth, not a denial of possession. St Paul in 2 Cor 4:10 says, "Poor ourselves we bring wealth to many, penniless we own the world." That is the way of Francis. He was no fool, he knew perfectly well that it is easier for a rich man to become poor than a poor man. The literally poor have no choice. When he stripped himself naked before the Bishop, renouncing his home, father, friends, everything, he stepped out into the world as rich as Adam before the Fall.

It is true that later he preached to the birds, called animals his brothers and sisters, sang that great poem to Creation which is one of the glories of the Franciscan tradition, extolling, as it does, the unity of God with his whole creation – but he lived in a world where literal poverty was as great a reality as on the streets of Calcutta today – or London for that matter – and was part of a Church which had the same struggle over possessions as the Church today. It is impossible to say whether Francis today would be more concerned with the problems of pollution and population or the many millions we are raising to save our cathedrals from falling down. What emerged in him was a profound distrust of money and possessions of any kind and a deep consciousness of God present in his creation.

In his deeper self Francis was aware of a world shot through with the glory and the presence of God. He was a romantic, a troubadour, a poet – and therefore a paradox, and it is largely in paradoxical terms that we can ever discern a Franciscan spirituality. That great lover of paradox, G. K. Chesterton, wrote a delightful biography of St Francis which got some of the facts wrong – but the ideas right. He says:

> Francis was not a lover of nature, properly under-
> stood a lover of nature is precisely what he was not.
> The phrase implies accepting the material universe as

a vague environment, a sort of sentimental pantheism
. . . For Francis nothing was ever in the background:
we might say his mind has no background, except perhaps, that Divine darkness out of which the Divine
love had called up every coloured creature one by one.
In a word, we talk about men who cannot see the
wood for the trees: St Francis was a man who didn't
want to see the wood for the trees – he wanted to see
each tree as a separate, almost a sacred thing. St
Francis was a mystic, but he believed in mysticism not
mystification. He was the enemy of all those mystics
who melt away the edges of things and dissolve an
entity with its environment.

The world in every possible expression of its being did not
merely remind him of God its creator, but identified him
with God present in his creation and, by a process of
exchange, shared it.

His love for Mankind

It is against this background that we might consider the
second facet of his spirituality – his love for mankind, or
more precisely his love for Christ as man, and, as a direct
and absolute consequence, his love of all mankind in
Christ. Everyone individually – whether it was the Pope,
the priest or the peasant, the sultan or the sinner – but in
particular the poor – whether they happened to be rich or
not. There are a number of popular devotions which are
said to spring from a Franciscan source, the Christmas crib,
the Stations of the Cross, the Angelus – all extolling the
Incarnation in one way or another. He understood the dignity conferred on man by the coming of Christ to share our
lives and instinctively acknowledged the divinity in man
as he also revered the humanity of Christ – who "for us and
for our salvation came down from heaven".

There was a glorious abandon in his love and care for

others, seeing them truly as his brothers and sisters, and his particular reverence for the poor acknowledged Christ's own identification with them. He wanted to be like Jesus, and to that end found vital meaning in the words of St Paul (2 Cor 8:9), "You know how generous our Lord Jesus Christ has been: he was rich yet for your sake he became poor so that through his poverty you might become rich."

The story of the leper makes the point. I suppose there could be an element of romantic illusion which gives a distance to the story – after all, few of us have ever seen a leper (though kissing a man or woman with AIDS might be a different matter) Kazartzakis in his penetrating novel on St Francis, *God's Pauper*, puts it more clearly. When Brother Leo tries to persuade Francis to avoid the leper coming towards him he replies, "There will be a leper on every road we take." The book then goes on to describe Francis meeting, embracing and kissing the leper whose lips, it says, were an oozing wound. Francis gathers the leper in his arms and carries him. Later, in bewilderment and joy, he says to Brother Leo, "This, Brother, is what I understand: all lepers, cripples, sinners: all these if you kiss them – O God forgive me for saying this – they all become Christ."

For Francis the exchange of love between God and man in Christ was absolute, as he has shared our humanity, so we have shared his divinity – and all mankind, personally, individually and absolutely were to be seen as Christ and honoured and served accordingly.

His love of God

It was one of his rich friends who gave Francis the opportunity for the deepest realisation of his union with Christ, which lies indeed at the heart of his spiritual life – his union with Christ crucified. He was offered the gift of a mountain, and perhaps only a truly poor man could freely accept so large a gift. Towards the end of his life Francis went to his mountain – a hermitage – to make a retreat. It was the

Feast of the Holy Cross. There was confusion in the Order, a conflict of goals, the leadership was no longer in his hands but had been taken over by a brother who was a powerful organiser and administrator – to the distress of those brothers who wanted to retain the simple lifestyle of Francis. He was in much physical pain and half blind. This time of prayer was to unify his life. At the beginning of his conversion he had prayed before the crucifix in San Damiano, and the crucified Christ had sent him out to rebuild his Church. It led to a life of poverty, preaching and prayer. Through it all there had lived in him a devotion to the Passion of Christ as the true point of our rebirth. It was this passion that he prayed now, with all the surrender of a lover for his beloved. Alone on the mountain, stretching out his arms as a cross it seems he was visited by angelic powers, and, lifted into union with Christ, the livid marks of the passion appeared in his hands, feet and side. When finally he returned they had to be bound up. The seal of his love and union with God is the stigmata. It could well be dismissed as induced by an ecstatic or explained away on psychological or emotional grounds – yet they are for those who know his life a logical and, one might say, necessary conclusion to it.

A spirituality for today

What then might constitute a valid Franciscan spirituality for today? Or how might we live a life toward God informed by the insights of the tradition of St Francis? I would like to conclude with a collection of thoughts which might offer a clue – but not much more.

One of the most striking sayings of Francis occurs in his *Canticle of the Sun*, which begins "Praise be to my Lord God in all his Creatures and especially our Brother the Sun. . . ." There is so much in it of praise of the created world that we can almost miss the concluding phrases composed when he was near death. "Praised be my Lord by those who pardon one another for his love's sake, for thou O Most Mighty shall give them a crown," and "Praised be my Lord by our Sister the Death of the Body from which no man escapeth." Death is the moment of truth, the uncomfortable yet glorifying truth which Francis discovered again and again all his life long. Death to his family when he stripped himself, death to his fear when he kissed the leper, death to possession, death to sin, death to self. His identification of himself with the death of Christ on the Cross meant liberation for the possession of the whole world in an eternal life of risen glory. It was the origin of the joy, which for those who experienced it was beyond anything they could imagine.

His honouring of priests, his protection of the Church, his fear of the insecure world which pins its hopes on buildings and power, his love of peace, and above all, his love of the poor, all sprang I think from this recognition. Francis is unique only in this; that he drew the whole of creation in all its infinite diversity of expression into an eternal and continual evolution of life and death.

Practically speaking this means that nothing is impossible. At one extreme a man or woman might live the life of a contemplative, a hermit, a monk or nun; at the other men and women will find their spiritual fulfilment with Francis as they give themselves to the care of alcoholics, drug addicts, prisoners, the deprived or victims of AIDS. And between them are men and women who in the context of their daily lives are equally inspired to embrace and share in the wonder of creation while giving themselves to overcoming the desolate wastes created by man through war, over-population, racial and social discrimination, pollution, selfishness, greed, pride, conflict, division, despair.

And this requires in us, as it did in Francis, a positive movement in heart and will, an act of recognition, a response, as Francis made it, to the prior action of God. Christ has already given us life – it is He who died, who speaks. So Paul says, "I live, yet not I but Christ liveth in me." This is a present fact, and it is the starting point which changes everything else. Everything we do is either an affirmation or a denial of this same truth. From the time of his conversion the whole life of Francis, it seems, in every detail, was an affirmation of the indwelling Christ, and alone accounts for his astonishing degree of liberation and freedom.

To be free in this way is to be free to recognise Christ in others – to see them in a new way. Francis really did see them as his brothers and sisters in whom, because Christ lived on earth, Christ still lived on earth.

It also made him free to possess the world – and therefore free from those things that tie us to the world; free to live always at the point of the world's need – as seen by God, not by man; free to recognise the proportion and truth as well as the pain and passion of events.

And finally, free to acknowledge a new community in love which shares a recognition of the redemptive power of God, beginning just where we are, with ourselves. The crown is for those who "pardon one another for his love's sake". Francis defines a path of peaceful reconciliation, a way of forgiveness that gives creative love new power in the world.

Franciscan life is never far from family life. Yet Francis distrusted the large fixed groups – there was always with him a sense of a family on the move, like gypsies, pilgrims, or a circus – and it excluded no-one at all.

I am conscious that what may be looked for is a technique, a manner of prayer, a tradition which could properly be labelled "Franciscan", and this may seem only a background or an environment.

The truth is that when the Third World has caught up with and passed the Second and First Worlds, man will remain impoverished by his greed and denial of God in creation. To share the poverty of Christ is to share the riches of Christ, and to live at the point of the reconciliation and redemption of man with God, which is the Cross. Just there, and it can be anywhere, is where the Franciscan spiritual tradition can be found alive in any one of us.

Addresses

Three Talks for Holy Week

THE KINGDOM, THE POWER, THE GLORY

St Bene't's Church, Cambridge. Holy Week, 1989

THE KINGDOM

Pilate then went back into his headquarters and summoned Jesus. "Are you the King of the Jews?" he asked. Jesus said, "Is that your own idea, or have others suggested it to you?" "What! am I a Jew?" said Pilate. "Your own nation and their chief priests have brought you before me. What have you done?" Jesus replied, "My kingdom does not belong to this world. If it did, my followers would be fighting to save me from arrest by the Jews. My kingly authority comes from elsewhere." "You are a king, then?" said Pilate. Jesus answered, " 'King' is your word. My task is to bear witness to the truth. For this was I born; for this I came into the world, and all who are not deaf to truth listen to my voice." Pilate said, "What is truth?" and with those words went out again to the Jews. "For my part," he said, "I find no case against him. But you have a custom that I release one prisoner for you at Passover. Would you like me to release the King of the Jews?" Again the clamour rose: "Not him; we want Barabbas!" (Barabbas was a bandit.)

Pilate now took Jesus and had him flogged; and the soldiers plaited a crown of thorns and placed it on his head, and robed him in a purple cloak. Then time after time they came up to him, crying, "Hail, King of the Jews!" and struck him on the face.

John 18:33-19:3

One of the most popular images of royalty in Britain is of a well preserved grandmother wearing a sensible tweed coat and a head-scarf eagerly watching a horse race. Or for that matter a very well preserved great-grandmother, rather more stylishly dressed, doing the same thing. Our queens are not expected to be regal all the time. It is true we also see her in a long stiff dress wearing, a little uneasily, a very large jewel encrusted, and clearly rather heavy, crown, escorted by ladies in waiting with glazed eyes and fixed expressions, as she adjusts her glasses to read a speech prepared for her by her Prime Minister, and over which she has almost no control at all.

The rôle of the Queen is largely ceremonial, and so will be that of the King when he succeeds her. Kings and queens in history are another matter – so are kings in Shakespeare and all the other image-formers that might fill our minds. Kings wear crowns, rule kingdoms, make laws, fight battles – have subjects. Kings have power and wealth, kings can decide for life and death. And kings also die.

That is the way kings used to be, but already, a hundred years ago, Lewis Carrol was suggesting that kings now have no more power than a pack of cards. "Off with her head," screamed the Queen – but Alice knew it was an empty threat. Perhaps before we approach this famous dialogue between Pilate and Jesus it would be as well to reflect on just how much of the old imagery we carry with us concerning kings – or Caesars, presidents and other symbols of the head of state.

There have been kings in the past who exercised such absolute authority, wielded an absolute power, and in our time the frightening abuse of such power has been demonstrated in Russia, Hungary, Haiti and elsewhere by men who could say with Pilate, "I have authority to release you and authority to destroy you." And destroy they did in fearful concentration camps, prisons, before firing squads, with poison, torture and a ruthless determination to kill. Such tyrant dictators were successors of tyrant Caesars, tyrant kings – they are nearer the model presented to us by Pilate, than the peace-loving, hard-working establishment figure peacefully preserving protocol, living a vanishing life in a vanishing world, wearing homely head-scarf or, rarely, a top-heavy crown brought out only to help her to look like the pictures on the pack of cards.

What are these two men like who face each other, Pilate and Jesus?

Pilate is the older of the two, a career man from Rome, baked a bit by the Palestinian sun, but nevertheless lighter skinned than Jesus. A married man, with a superstitious wife, while he himself probably had the background of conventional acceptance of the gods and a grudging sense that they hadn't helped him as much as they might. He is conscious of his position and authority but knows he could be criticised as weak. He will dodge a decision if he can or push it on to someone else, as he does in this case. He's a long way from Rome but Rome has a long arm, and Caesar is all powerful. And that is the kingdom he represents. Rome rules, not only in Palestine but all over Europe, an empire that has already reached Britain. Roman roads, Roman rules and laws, Roman soldiers, Roman customs. Rome, tolerant of minorities so long as they never challenge Roman authority, never challenge Caesar. For those who do the ruthless Roman system answers with justice, imprisonment, death – and the string of crosses outside the town are a grim reminder of the consequences of insurrection.

Is Jesus, then, just one more challenge to Roman authority, a rebel, or rabble-rouser, of which at that time there were many. One more trouble on the eve of a Jewish feast, something to clear out of the way before we shut down for the Jewish festival and a quiet weekend for the Romans. Perhaps – but we see it from a Christian point of view, written up thirty or more years after the event.

There is no need to doubt the accuracy of it. The story, from our point of view, is so important that essentials would be preserved by Jewish storytellers with conscious attention to detail. After all, we can remark with clarity significant incidents of our lives which happened in the 60s.

But we might also treasure this dialogue between Pilate and Jesus because it comes as the final declaration by Jesus of all that he had said before, throughout his three years ministry, about the Kingdom. For Pilate this idea that Jesus is a king is just the inevitable claim of an upstart rebel, a challenge to Caesar that could hardly be taken seriously and deserves nothing more than a good hiding, a flogging which, fearfully painful, was nevertheless a fairly frequent and quite unremarkable punishment, meant only as a strong hint not to cause trouble by making ridiculous claims that disturbed the peace and encouraged violent followers.

For Jesus it is another matter altogether. He is thirty-three, probably at the height of his power – physically, mentally. The challenge to Pilate as they stand man to man, lies not in anything he says but what he is, what he has become. What lies behind Pilate is centuries of developing Roman power all culminating and fulfilled in Caesar whom he represents. While what lies behind Jesus is a comparatively short life of gradual discovery and growing realisation about himself and God whom he speaks of as his father, the realisation of a relationship expressed in prayer and such a profound unity of purpose that he and his father are absolutely one. God speaks through him, he speaks for God, God is in Him, He is in God. Even the name of God who said "I Am" is one he dares to apply to himself. He inhabits God's world, which he calls God's Kingdom.

That world of unapproachable majesty, absolute justice and truth – that eternal world of which the Jews hardly dared speak – that was the world Jesus called the Kingdom.

It was *that* world which Jesus had come to know in *this* world – and not just to know, but to claim as his own, be at one with God in it, sharing His divinity, as readily as he lived in this world, and shared the humanity of us all.

So these men face each other, share the same humanity, are governed by the same human laws and fears, the need for sleep, food, friendship, the need to recognise success by which mankind can live with some integrity – accepting laws of love, trust, confidence and compassion.

It might be that facing each other, man to man, they recognise something to respect, caught as they are in the constrictions of a framework that demanded the use of words, and the exercise of an authority imposed on them both by the human circumstance.

But they are hopelessly at cross purposes. Pilate hadn't *been* there when Jesus first appeared on the scene saying, "The Kingdom of Heaven is at hand." He hadn't *heard* all the parables, listened to all the teaching which again and again set out to explain the Kingdom, stories that took the same material world of ordinary men and women known only too well to a man like Pilate and used it to illustrate the total reversal of values which marked the presence of the Kingdom, that made this world one with that eternal world which is the ultimate reality, and of which this, for all its apparent substance, is only a shadow. So the Kingdom of Heaven is a world where "the blind look in a mirror, and love looks back at them", cripples leap, the poor are rich, and the rich poor, where power is exercised in weakness rather than strength, and the King is recognised only by his humility which he wears with unconscious glory. Poor Pilate, he'd heard nothing of it, and might well have been none the wiser if he had – after all the Pharisees had heard and far from understanding were, for all their religious fervour, so caught up in the world of Pilate, with law and traditions, that they determined to crush the revolutionary idea and found Jesus a fearful threat that must be destroyed, using Pilate to see it happened. After all, they knew about kings and could speculate on the restoration of a David as hopelessly as those sad royalists in Russia hoped for the restoration of a Romanoff.

So Pilate says, "Are you a king?" But how could Jesus explain a whole world of spiritual reality? The answer was bound to be ambiguous. Best to say as he does, "my kingly authority comes from elsewhere".

Pilate's anxiety and fear increase and he threatens Jesus with his ability to release or destroy him. In fact the outcome is inevitable; Jesus is finally condemned, convicted, crowned and crucified, and the ultimate ambiguity is the title above his head which Pilate refuses to alter, "This is Jesus, the King of the Jews." Or is it the crown – even a crown of thorns?

Jesus had instructed his followers to pray, "Thy kingdom come, on earth as in heaven." Was this, then, the true earthly coronation of the King? That would certainly be all one with the teaching. Pilate has his memorial above *His* head. It reads "crucified under Pontius Pilate", and has been repeated daily in Christian churches for two thousand years.

And what of us, what will our memorial be, we who watch and wait in Holy Week? I have prayed many times "Thy kingdom come" – would I recognise the King – if he comes to the door with a ring in his ear and torn jeans begging for bread? Can the Kingdom come in the compassion of a police officer patrolling the back areas of an industrial town, is the King welcoming his citizens at the job centre, or the addiction centre, or helping the birth of a baby whose mother has AIDS?

It is easy to condemn Pilate but how much of the Pharisee is in me?

Most of the world knows as little about the Kingdom as they did. How seriously, in my own heart, do I feel for the values of the King; or really to live as if the Kingdom could be the reality, and the materialistic and all too human world the shadow, and only the beginning of the beginning. In the play about C. S. Lewis which tells the story of his passion, the death of his wife from cancer after only three years of Kingdom happiness, there is a fantasy in the style of Narnia, a huge window-door at the end of his library which swings open – and the young son of his wife Joy Davidman, steps through it into the shining reality which is always there for us to see, once our eyes have become accustomed to the true world of the Kingdom on earth, our ears tuned to the voice of Jesus and our hearts open to the radiant love of God which welcomes us as being of this world, and yet not of this world, citizens of the Kingdom, loyal subjects of the King.

One of the barriers to understanding, one source of a blindness which prevents us from recognising, really seeing or even catching a glimpse of the Kingdom in this world is the false conviction of permanence that leads us to cry, as they did in Egypt, "Oh King live for ever." We all tend to act, think, plan for much of our lives as if we too will live for ever: but kingdoms rise and fall, "The Captains and the Kings depart." Our thinking is related too readily to an eternal "Now", and, like misers, we hoard our days, and all the material means of enjoying them. When in very truth the only enjoyment can come from knowing they are *not* permanent, and that here we have no abiding city. To enter the Kingdom and truly be a part of it is to recognise the transient for what it is worth, no matter how substantially it seems to be represented – and the eternal for all it is, no matter how fleetingly or rarely we know it in our hearts and minds.

The dying thief discovered it, almost too late. "Lord remember me when you come into your kingdom." Do we, like him, live in Pilate's world, robbing creation for ends that are acquisitive, selfish, and which, no matter how successful we are or possessive we are, have no future for us here? We leave them all, the possessive love of things or persons, power and profit. All such power is in the end such petty crime – and we end up like the penitent thief, we end up also like Jesus in his death. To recognise the

Kingdom of Heaven is to be like Jesus in his eternal and everlasting glory. As St Paul says – we shall reign with Him.

Do you remember the song in West *Side Story?*

> It's only just out of reach
> Down the block, on the beach
> Under a tree
> I've got a feeling there's a miracle due
> Bound to come true
> Coming to me.

He was singing of Love. The song of the Passion is Love Unknown – the singer is the King of Love, and the elusive reality that Jesus represented before Pilate, and for which He died is the Kingdom of Love.

It is for you also he says, "Today you will be with me in Paradise."

Let the last words be those of R. S. Thomas in a much quoted poem:

> It's a long way off but inside it
> There are quite different things going on:
> Festivals at which the poor man
> Is king and the consumptive is
> Healed: mirrors In which the blind look
> at themselves and love looks at them
> Back; and industry is for mending
> The bent bones and the minds fractured
> By life. It's a long way off, but to get
> There takes no time and admission
> Is free, if you will purge yourself
> Of desire, and present yourself with
> Your need only and the simple offering
> Of your faith, green as a leaf.

THE POWER

In the sixth month the angel Gabriel was sent from God to a town in Galilee called Nazareth, with a message for a girl betrothed to a man named Joseph, a descendant of David; the girl's name was Mary. The angel went in and said to her, "Greetings most favoured one! The Lord is with you." But she was deeply troubled by what he said and wondered what this greeting might mean. Then the angel said to her, "Do not be afraid, Mary, for God has been gracious to you; you shall conceive and bear a son, and you shall give him the name Jesus. He will be great; He will bear the title 'Son of the Most High'; the Lord God will give Him the throne of his ancestor David, and he will be King over Israel for ever; His reign shall never end." "How can this be?" said Mary, "I am still a virgin." The angel answered, "The Holy Spirit will come upon you, and the power of the Most High will overshadow you; and for that reason the holy child to be born will be called 'Son of God'. Moreover your kinswoman Elizabeth has herself conceived a son in her old age; and she who is reputed barren is now in her sixth month, for God's promises can never fail." "Here am I," said Mary, "I am the Lord's servant; as you have spoken, so be it." Then the angel left her.

Luke 1:26-38

"Do you refuse to speak to me?" said Pilate. "Surely you know that I have authority to release you, and I have authority to crucify you?" "You would have no authority at all over me," Jesus replied, "if it had not been granted you from above; and therefore the deeper guilt lies with the man who handed me over to you."

John 19:10-11

187

Power, in human terms, is most frequently and familiarly related to the rise and fall of nations. As a boy I was left in no doubt that the British Empire was the greatest power in the world, an Empire boldly coloured red on the map and on which the sun never set. What I was not told was that, in fact, the sun was already setting, and quite fast, in historical terms, and that at the same time other powers were ascending. So we came in time to talk of the "Great Powers", of "Power Blocks". The principal evidence of power was the possession of weapons of destruction and the economic resources to build and increase them. The power of the atom bomb, nuclear power, widely claimed only to be held in vast supply for the preservation of peace. Britain became a second class power – America and Russia were *the* "Great Powers". Former powers who used their strength in war and had been defeated, notably Germany and Japan, ceased to be powers at all in the military sense, but there always remained the possibility of economic power, and that is exactly what has happened.

The futility of mutual self-destruction has slowly been recognised and the appalling consequences accepted. Nuclear power, one of the most outstanding discoveries of man, it was thought, can now be directed to creative use, only to discover that without great care its misuse can endanger our whole environment, as can so much else.

Scientific power is a two-edged sword. So the power game becomes a means of unlimited possibilities for good, and at the same time a terrifying threat even to the point of annihilation, in which the crude use of arms on an extensive scale, as in the war in Vietnam or the tragic and heroic loss of life in the Falklands war, is only the most obvious parade of strength. More terrible still in many ways is the ruthless use of national power against the defenceless as in the June 4th massacre in Tiananmen Square, the suppression of black South Africans, or the threat to the Balkan states.

Supporting such crude power – and it is reflected

throughout society in its use for good or ill down to the
simplest minor official in any organisation – is power of
another kind, the power of the human mind, of ideas,
power translated into the written, printed, spoken word,
the power of the public orator, the loud-hailer, the television screen and radio. From *The Communist Manifesto* and
the writings of Marx and Lenin to the speeches of Lech
Walesa in the shipyard of Gdansk, or the plays of Vaclav
Havel in Prague, the face of Europe has been fundamental-
ly changed in the past seventy years, and the power of their
words, and many many more, have played a profoundly
significant part in it . For they have articulated the needs
and hopes of the people, the "Common Man" as he is so
frequently represented in the plays of Bertholt Brecht. The
people who in the end cannot tolerate tyranny and the misuse of power and are encouraged to find a power in themselves the greater strength, the power of an ideal of justice
and truth, honesty and generosity, the power of human life
and human love. The suffering of the oppressed is
translated into the power of human will suffering for a
righteous cause, suffering for humanity within the human
situation, finding dignity, honour and a strength which
cannot be defeated. The records of the Jews in the ghetto of
Warsaw, of Dietrich Bonhoeffer in Germany, of Sakharov in
Russia, testify to this truth – but there are millions more
with names unknown who stand beside them. And so does
Jesus, as he stands before Pilate.

There is something of the bully in Pilate as he says, "I
have power to release you, and power to destroy you."

The reply of Jesus seems ambiguous, "You would have
no power unless it was given you from above." Does he
mean from Caesar – certainly Pilate's exercise of power is
derived entirely from his place in the system – he is very
much a part of the power structure. Or is Jesus also affirm-
ing the source of power which is common to them both –
the power of God? To misuse that power is certainly

the greater sin – for essentially it is the sin against the Holy Spirit.

Once more they are at cross purposes. The power of Pilate is, in the end, powerless against Jesus. His human body can indeed be destroyed but He himself cannot be, for the power of Jesus is the power of God. Reflecting on Jesus, the writer of the Fourth Gospel declares, "All things were made by Him. In Him was life. The Word became flesh and dwelt among us."

So, we are reminded, it was also in the beginning with Mary, and the angel declared, "The Power of the Most High will overshadow you" – and so it was, and we beheld his glory. Only our eyes were unaccustomed to glory in human form. The power of God in a man, among all humanity. True power in human flesh and blood. Blood of our blood, and life of our life. So Pilate can threaten the all too human Jesus by a display of power, power to kill the human body. This has always been a sign of human power, power of Cain which is recorded, for instance, every week in the mutilated bodies of Northern Ireland, or by a political prisoner, saying before he was shot down, "You can only kill me once, and then what can you do? You can destroy my body, but you cannot destroy me."

The true strength of Jesus lies in his knowledge of the power given him from above. The power that rested on him at his baptism, the power that drove him into the wilderness where, before his ministry had begun, he met the Pilates of this world and overcame them by the power of the Spirit. That Spirit which he claimed for himself in the synagogue – "The Spirit of the Lord is upon me," he read. That same Spirit was declared in the power of his preaching, the power of his healing hands, the power of forgiving love.

That was also the power which could move men and women to faith, the surrender of their lives. The power to transform others into the likeness of gods. By that power, the demoniac was given back his mind, and sat calmly, side by side with Jesus, the lame walked, the blind saw. This was the power of compassion which in his humanity led him to tears for Lazarus and also gave Lazarus back his life.

For Jesus all this power of mind and spirit was contained in the same human form which is ours and His. Of all creation there is nothing more wonderful than this, the human body capable of infinite variety, every possible variation of beauty, containing potential for strength and subtlety which are endless. And yet in the end vulnerable to pain, suffering and death. Vulnerable to human power. And this too He shares. Yet this mortality had, in Him, already put on immortality: For Jesus death is indeed "but the gate to life immortal" – and the power no man can take from Him. Perhaps even Pilate is dimly conscious of being up against impossible odds, as he bluffs and blunders his way out of an awkward situation even against his own better judgement.

On the night before he died, Jesus spoke in a mysterious way to the disciples and with bewildered and fear-fuddled faces they looked at one another and asked themselves, "What does he mean?" At one point he seemed to be confiding that he intended making a bid for power – and in their confused misunderstanding a squabble breaks out as to who will get ministerial office in the new administration. So what did they make of his promise of power, the power not of swords but of the Spirit.

"If I go," he said, "your advocate will come. When he comes he will condemn the world, and show where wrong and right and judgement lie. He is the Spirit of truth who will guide you into all truth." It was hard for them to understand, and when it came to the crunch they all forsook him and fled. It is different for us, and there is less excuse, for we live on the other side of the Resurrection – and share the mystery of God's Love. We also share the mystery of His Power.

There is a Pilate on every path I tread. In government or education, in civil life and political life. There are fathers who act like Pilate in their families, petty officials who hide behind the little authority they wield. We meet it in schools and hospitals, colleges and councils, shops and offices.

There is a danger from Pharisees, too, both in the Church and outside it – and it might include me.

My only strength lies in standing alongside Jesus, saying with Him, "You would have no power except it was given you from above." My power is the power of Jesus, of the Word made flesh, the power of His Spirit.

How might I wonder at the mystery of God. who became man for me – that I might be God with Him, in the power of the same Spirit.

Let the last word be with John Donne:

> Wilt thou love God as he thee! then digest,
> My Soule, this wholsome meditation,
> How God the Spirit, by Angels waited on
> In heaven, doth make his Temple in thy brest.
> The Father having begot a Sonne most blest,
> And still begetting, (for he ne'r begonne)
> Hath deign'd to chuse thee by adoption,
> Coheire to "his glory", and Sabaths endlesse rest;
> And as a robb'd man, which by search doth finde
> His stolne stuffe sold, must lose or buy'it againe:
> The Sonne of glory came downe, and was slaine,
> Us whom he'had made, and Satan stolne, to unbinde.
> 'Twas much, that man was made like God before,
> But, that God should be made like man, much more.

THE GLORY

As soon as I think of Glory I think also of Michael Ramsey. A very large and rather clumsy man, a shock of white hair, a sort of bat-like energy in his arms and hands as he tries to express himself, hesitant sometimes in speech as the most precise word is searched for, lengthy pauses, and then pouncing on a word and, finding it so right, repeating it with relish. Eyebrows flashing signals of delight, eyes bright with the discovery and his whole body responding so that from his smile to his shoes he embodied a sort of radiance. "Glory" was a word he relished in just such a way, and its significance is all the more important for us, because Michael Ramsey was one of those rare men and women who had in a long life put on through prayer and the integrity of his life towards God something of that wonder which is not only of this world alone, but that world of Glory which belongs to God.

Glory is a word that belongs to the people of God. We would exclude no-one in the world from sharing in that understanding for after all Glory itself is not exclusive. There is a glory of the sun and moon, the stars and all the created firmament. There is a glory of the spring and the first flowers, a glory we can encourage, nurture and protect but could never create ourselves, it is all given by God. There is a glory in the human face and form and whether men know it or not, we declare God's creative love in our lives. As Hopkins has so happily said it:

> I say more: the just man justices;
> keeps grace: that keeps all his going graces,
> Acts in God's eyes what in God's eye he is –
> Christ – for Christ plays in ten thousand places,
> Lovely in limbs, and lovely in eyes not his
> To the Father through the features of men's faces.

Yet only those who are seeking to surrender their lives to the mystery of God, to know in this world the ultimate glory of eternal life, only those who through prayer and faith, through love and pain, through the confusions of our common vocation to be Christ in the world, will find they also have eyes to see beyond sight, glimpse beyond the veil of substance the eternal realities. We live in the brutal reality of a world capable of infinite beauty, capable of reflecting the ultimate glory but subject to men who destroy the rain forests, cover the ground with concrete, make money their only strength, and cash value their only proof of power. We are crowded around with a majority of people who are blind to true beauty, and can catch no glimpse of glory. The paradox is that the vast muddy pool in its stillness reflects the stars.

In the middle of such conflict where will we find the God of Glory?

The word itself has an important history for me. It sprang as much as anything from the searching of a prophet to describe the indescribable. Ezekiel, the priest, had seen with the inward eye of prayer and with the power of the Spirit, something of the majesty of God. The God of Abraham, Isaac and Jacob, the God who spoke to Moses in the bush and on the mountain (and you will remember that so close was the encounter with the blazing Majesty that when Moses came down from the mountain, though he didn't know it, his face also burned so brightly that they put a cloth over it out of reverence and awe – for Moses had seen God, face to face). This is the God who went before the people in a pillar of cloud. But Ezekiel has seen more than that and he tries to describe it.

> Above the heads of the living creatures was, as it were, a vault glittering like a sheet of ice, awe-inspiring, stretched over their heads above them. Under the vault their wings were spread straight out, touching one another, while one pair covered the body of each.
>
> Above the vault over their heads there appeared, as if it were, a sapphire in the shape of a throne, and high

above all, upon the throne, a form in human likeness. I saw what might have been brass glowing like fire in a furnace from the waist upwards; and from the waist downwards I saw what looked like fire with encircling radiance. Like a rainbow in the clouds on a rainy day was the sight of that encircling radiance; it was like the appearance of the glory of the Lord.

Ez 1:22,23,26-28

This is the language of a priest, a visionary, in a contemporary world we would speak of fantasy, even of science fiction, and it is all summed up as Glory.

Now the Hebrew word Ezekiel used, "Glory", in fact describes something a little different. Its primary meaning is weight and substance. A man of weight or substance is KABOD – glorious. His external appearance and wealth would reflect it – KABOD, GLORY – would command respect from his fellow men, and that respect too was glory or honour. So wealth, dignity, noble bearing, honour, all are a reflection of glory. And to that Ezekiel adds *brightness*.

Bit by bit these ideas of glory became seen as a future possession, something that belonged to the great age of the Messiah, and for us that means the age of Jesus. Against that background the record of the age of Jesus and his followers in the New Testament suddenly begins to sparkle, and like flashes of brilliance the word glory appears again and again and mostly notably in St John's Gospel describing the life of Jesus, and in St Paul as he tries to say what the effect of that has been in the first age of the Christians; the Hebrew word is replaced by a Greek word, and enriched. It was understandable that the richest image Ezekiel could find was one which captured oriental splendour, the great man of worth, the man to be honoured, and whose honourable deeds were reflected in his beauty and the honour he conferred on others.

Now that too is enriched as it becomes focused on one man, on Jesus. Nothing is too great for him and glory is made greater still as it is employed to describe the indescribable, the heaven of heavens, the awesome and awe inspiring Godhead revealed in all the humanity of a man. So his birth is one which identifies him even with poverty, obscurity, with all the uncertainties of not being a legitimate birth. He is born under circumstances that are provisional, accompanied by violence which forces his parents to flee with him for their lives, something with which countless refugee families can identify.

Yet at the same time he is surrounded by glory. The noblemen of wealth who came to worship him as a King exactly fit the bill and could have been fitted out by Ezekiel, and though there were humble shepherds as well, they were given the message by a choir of angels. In fact from the start it had been made clear that he would be great. "Son of the Most High", King over Israel – so the angels sing, "Glory to God in the Highest" and John in his gospel echoes it, "We beheld his glory, glory as of the only begotten of the Father."

From then onwards in St John's Gospel it is glory all the way, emphasising an ever increasing contrast between the revelation in Jesus of the transcendent glory of God and the all too human, vulnerable, misunderstood, and finally most violently rejected, Glory of Man. There was a glory that went unrecognised in his preaching, teaching and healing ministry, in his love of the poor and the life of homelessness he shared with them. From the start he said that theirs was the Kingdom of Heaven – and as King he welcomed them.

But the antagonism closed in and he began to pray, "Father save me from this hour," yet added, "No, it was for this I came to this hour. Father, glorify thy name." And the Father answered "I have glorified it, and will glorify it again." So the path to Calvary was to be the path of Glory.

It was hard to understand. How could the prince, the great man, the honourable man, so humble himself? It was against all prophecy, against reason, common sense, against every demand for loyalty he might make on his disciples – for that matter on us. But he pressed on, and when they wouldn't understand what he was saying he turned to action – and like a slave went round, washing their feet. In a silence broken only by the impetuous Peter, the message at last got home, at any rate to Judas. So *this* was the path of glory – and in disgust he swept out, and sold Jesus. The path of glory had a price as well. Thirty pieces of silver. The door is barely closed when Jesus knowing only too well what has happened and that his fate is sealed bursts out, "*Now* is the Son of Man glorified, and in Him God is glorified. If God is glorified in him, God will also glorify him in himself and he will glorify him *now.*"

For Jesus the hour has come, and He turns it all into a prayer, a prayer which in some ways is at the heart of all prayer. The prayer of Glory, the prayer which declares the place we have in the heart of Jesus, the prayer which lifts us in his heart into the heavenly places where He ever liveth to make intercession for us, the prayer that unites heaven and earth, that makes one, for ever, the perfect humanity and the perfect divinity of Jesus, the Son who is always and for ever one with the Father, the prayer which penetrates the mystery of our own union with God in Jesus.

So He says, "Father the hour has come, glorify thy Son that the Son may glorify thee. I have glorified you on the earth having done the work you gave me to do. And now O Father glorify me in your presence with the glory I had with you before the world began."

And there is more than that, he continues, "the glory which thou gavest me I have given them."

How well do we understand this? Remember, this was his last prayer before the Cross. He left praying and was soon surrounded by soldiers, spears, swords – and Judas, with the Judas kiss. So there was glory in betrayal from Judas, and then denial from Peter, glory in the stripping, the flogging, the deep gashes, the flowing blood, glory in

the soldiers' mockery, glory in the nails, glory in the crown
of thorns. And no one to help. " God, he cried, why have
you forsaken me." How strangely true was the ancient
prophet when he said:

> Look down from heaven and behold
> From the heights where thou dwellest holy and glorious
> Where is thy zeal, thy valour,
> Thy burning and tender love.

But the same prophet had already said more, much more
than he could ever have understood of the path of glory,
which is the path of pain:

> He grew up before the Lord like a young plant
> whose roots are in parched ground;
> he had no beauty, no majesty to draw our eyes
> no grace to make us delight in him;
> his form, disfigured, lost all the likeness of a man,
> his beauty changed beyond human semblance.
> He was despised, he shrank from the sight of men,
> tormented and humbled by suffering;
> we despised him, we held him of no account,
> a thing from which men turn away their eyes.
>
> _Isaiah 53:2–3_

So the path of Glory led to death – and death to life.

And what of us? St Paul leaves us in no doubt – and he
is a good witness. A man who had known as a Pharisee the
old dispensation to the letter – and then had himself put on
glory, trodden the same path as Jesus, flogging, imprisonment, starvation, shipwreck, homelessness and in spite of
that, writing to Corinth, he speaks of the "Gospel of the
glory of Christ" and says, "We never lose heart." And more
than that he is bold to say, "We proclaim Christ Jesus as
Lord and ourselves your servants – for God has caused his
light to shine within us to give the light of revelation – the
revelation of the glory of God in the face of Jesus Christ."

For St Paul had discovered he could gaze on God and

needed no veil over his face to hide the brightness of that encounter. And it can be true for you, if you will walk with Christ his path of the passion, the path he trod for your sins and mine – then receive and share his forgiving love and be made free to know his glory in your life. For Paul says, "Because for us there is no veil over the face we all reflect in a mirror the glory of the Lord, thus we are transfigured into his likeness from glory to glory." Such is the influence of the Lord who is the Spirit. But it can be years. That transformation may take a lifetime.

Let the last word be with the last poem of George Herbert, for in Christ – thine also is the Kingdom, and the Power, and the Glory, for ever and ever.

> King of glorie, King of peace,
> With the one make warre to cease;
> With the other blesse Thy sheep, Thee to love,
> In Thee to sleep.
> Let not Sinne devour Thy fold,
> Bragging that thy bloud is cold;
> That Thy death is also dead,
> While his conquests dayly spread;
> That Thy flesh hath lost his food,
> And Thy Crosse is common wood.
> Choke him, let him say no more,
> But reserve his breath in store,
> Till Thy conquests and his fall
> Make his sighs to use it all;
> And then bargain with the winde
> To discharge what is behinde.

The Death of Jesus

The University Church, Cambridge. Lent 1989

Jesus – His Death

There is a prayer addressed to the Virgin Mary, which is said, I should think, more frequently than any other prayer except the Lord's Prayer. It concludes, "Pray for us sinners now and at the hour of our death." We cannot escape the fact that these are indeed the two most important moments in our lives, and the one thing we all have in common, indeed the only two moments of which we can ever be absolutely certain. We don't know when we will die, we do know it is unavoidable.

So as we set out to consider the death of Jesus, one starting point might be a recognition of the way we think of our own. St Francis could be ecstatic about it and sing, "Praised be my Lord by our Sister the Death of the Body from which no man escapeth" – and clearly looked forward to it joyfully. It's not the way everyone approaches it.

Someone said recently that America is the only nation which regards death as an option! It may be true. There is a cruel satire on the American way of death in Evelyn Waugh's *The Loved One* with its description of "Whispering Glades" in California, a park where golden gates lead to an opulent funeral parlour. There, in the hands of Mr Joyboy, the mortician, the body is painted up, dressed up, and finally propped up on a couch in a beautifully decorated drawing room where his friends may come and visit with him, for all the world as if he were still alive. It is a stark contrast to the other side of Hollywood which has recently held up the mirror to fantasy rather than life, to a world in which death is repeatedly seen as a violent flourish of conflict and power. But then, we do live in an age of eruptive and terrible violence. What, after all, has the death of Jesus to say about the brutal murder of a taxi driver in Belfast, shot repeatedly while he was watching the television with his family – the sixteenth death in a month; another sectarian killing between Protestants and Catholics.

There is another recent film, the last made by John Houston, one of the great directors, and the film he said he had always wanted to make. Dying from cancer and wondering if he could finish it, it is based on a short story by James Joyce called The *Dead.* His daughter Angelica played the lead, a middle-aged woman who tells her husband for the first time of a youthful romance; a young man who literally died for love of her, and had no wish to live without her. She falls asleep, her husband Gabriel looks out of the window, where snow is falling. The book says:

> His eyes filled with tears. He had never felt like that towards any woman, but he knew that such a feeling must be love. The tears gathered more thickly in his eyes, and in the partial darkness he imagined he saw the form of a young man standing under a dripping tree.

(The girl had been forbidden to see him; the young man, who was dying of tuberculosis, had come to stand outside her house and say goodbye – it was raining, it killed him.) It continues:

> Other forms were near. His soul had approached that region where dwell the vast hosts of the dead. He was conscious of, but could not apprehend, that wayward and flickering existence. His own identity was fading out into a grey impalpable world; the solid world itself, which these dead had one time reared and lived in, was dissolving and dwindling.

That captures the sense of vague uncertainty and longing which characterises the deepest feelings of some people about death. We might indeed die for love, but that in no way of necessity lifts the curtain of perception on the uncertainty of what lies beyond death, for so many it remains Gabriel's "impalpable world". Or worse – or nothing – "You go step by step into the dark, the movement itself is the only truth,"says a dying actor in another film about death (by Ingmar Bergman – *The Face)*. So how does the death of Jesus help us to recognise the truth about our own death?

Beginning with God

St Paul says, "In Adam all die." I suppose I should bring him up to date and say, "In Adam and Eve all die!" For all humanity death is the ultimate crisis, and has been from the beginning of time and will be to the end of time. But beyond that is God, who is the beginning and end of time. Our understanding of death, and most particularly the death of Jesus, depends on our awareness and acceptance of this in the deepest part of our being. To understand death we first have to know, or want to know, the source of life. God the timeless, the eternal, the Creator of all things, who yet knows us at the level of profound and personal intimacy, every part of his creation and every person, and you, and me. Impossible to believe? Yes, very nearly, but any idea of God short of that would be inadequate and leave many more unanswerable questions.

At the very heart of this great creation story, at the very centre of history, is the event which makes sense of it all for us. The birth of Jesus. As historical an event as yours or mine, having a date and time and place. If the wise men had come armed with a Polaroid they could have taken an instant picture of Him. This creator God, who like a father or mother, has an intimate personal knowledge and relationship with each one of us, was born into our world, became one of us, another Adam, flesh of our flesh and blood of our blood. The mystery of God made evident in man. Jesus claimed God as His Father and calls us to do the same, makes us one with Him in the same family. This, he says, is what God is like. "I and my Father are one thing. If you have seen me you have seen my Father." Confusing?

Difficult? Yes, it can be. If the first act of faith leads us to the Eternal God, the second demands that we say, "I believe in Jesus, God and Man."

Jesus – born to die

Jesus shared our life and our death. He came to die. St Paul says, "'Bearing the human likeness, revealed in human shape, he humbled himself for us and in obedience accepted even death." In this respect he was no different from any of us. Then what makes the difference? There is a cynical remark going round that we are all suffering from a terminal sickness called life: it would be more accurate to say we are all suffering from a terminal sickness called sin. All of us, the whole of humanity, irrespective of race, colour, class, nationality, creed or anything. All the Adams and Eves, except one. All share this common fact, except Jesus, who, it says, "made himself sin for us, he who knew no sin"– tarred with the same brush.

Sin is a theological word. It describes the breakdown in relationship between mankind and God. Sin is not necessarily crime, though it may be. Crime describes a breakdown in the laws and rules made by man for the welfare of society, whether you believe in God or not. There are laws that were given by God as well, laws which Jesus obeyed, but also redefined. There is, he said, only one law, the law of God, the law of Love. It is because of his continued love of his creation and his people that Jesus came, that is why He was born, and why He died. So He defined it, "Love the Lord your God with all your heart and mind and soul and strength. That is the first law, the second is, Love your neighbour as you love yourself." Nothing less.

Sin is the denial of that love. The sin of Adam and Eve was to give in to the temptation to be like God himself, to be as good as God, know as much as he knows, exercise his power, and never die. Well, there is nothing new in that, it

203

is as prevalent today as then. To control, to dominate by power, if necessary use violence to secure it, to act as if we have all the time in the world to fulfil our plans, that can be as true in a family with a tyrannical father, a school with a bullying teacher as well as an international business or a nation.

Religious sects do it in the name of God, and we can find traces of it in each one of us. Sin is rooted in a failure to love ourselves aright – and so we not only fail to respond to God's love (and all love is initiated by Him), but our failure creates a barrier of blindness, and deafness between us and him. Something which only He can remove because he alone can still see, hear, understand, forgive, love.

Not least of the consequences of sin is an arrogance and self-deception which leads us as Christians to believe that, like God, we know in some absolute way the difference between good and evil, as if we have cornered the know-ledge of right and wrong. It shows in our attitude to death – not our own, but of other people. There are few sins more dangerous than taking to ourselves a right which belongs to God alone, the right to judge his people.

So from the beginning there was the association of sin with death – "the reward of sin" as the Bible would have it – and there are even some who dare to say who deserved it and who didn't.

Jesus was born to change that. God in His love for us took action to restore us to all he meant us to be when He first made us. It was a rescue operation to save us from our sinful condition, break down the barrier we had created. This divine intervention meant that Jesus could claim kin-ship with us and we with him. There never was a barrier between Jesus and the Father. He called us his brothers and sisters. He had a claim on us, and we on Him. He alone could love back, with the same absolute love of God the Father. Love for love. To do that He was exposed to all the hazards of the human situation.

The Dying of Jesus

I recently heard, on the radio, that one baby in every hundred is a premature birth, sometimes just a handful of baby, struggling for life. Jesus could have been like that. He grew up in a Palestine as critically political as it is today, was regarded as a troublemaker by the authorities, travelling light with a small band of followers, only to be betrayed by a traitor in his group who all, in any case, deserted him when he was arrested. Tried on a trumped-up charge by his religious authorities, he was executed by the civil authorities in the customary manner. It was brutal but in no way unusual. It is important to remember that this was a very ordinary death. Millions have died even more brutally. We live in a violent age and in any case there are other ways of dying, more prolonged, MS, cancer, AIDS, and all the rest. As "one of us" his death was just like yours or mine will be. He stopped breathing.

So What is the Meaning of this Death for Us?

This man, this Adam, was the one person who at the end of His life could offer back to God all he had been, in absolute perfection. An offering of perfect human, bodily love and heart and soul, mind and spirit. Offering His life, even, we can say, His life blood. This victim of violence offering the very things we all know so well, the consequences of sin. He knew what sin can do, better than any of us. Only someone who had never sinned, never given in to temptation (though He had known *that* well enough) could know what sin is like, what destruction sin really brings. So He accepted the destruction in his own body.

What He offered to God was not His death, but His life. He had knowledge of human life from beginning to end, childhood, teenager, youth, preacher, teacher, lover, in a way far more complete than we can ever know. We, in famous and familiar words are only "living and partly living". He came that we might have life, abundant life. That is what he gave to God; that is why his life blood was running down his body to make a pool of blood on the ground, like the pool of blood on the floor in front of the telly where the shot taxi driver lay dying. Jesus took on himself all the blood that has ever been spilt. Remember all those war memorials, all the young blood given for King or Queen and Country? So much waste. Martin Stephen's moving collection of war poems is called *Never Such Innocence*. It is just that innocence that Jesus offered for us: goodness to goodness, love to love, not for worldly kingdoms, but to establish a new territory of love in his world. He called it the Kingdom of Heaven.

The Meaning for Me

How can this mean something to us? Start again with his humanity. On the night before he died he said, "Greater love has no man than this, that he lay down his life for his friends. You are my friends. "Jesus knew about the death of friends. There was Lazarus. Jesus wept for his love of Lazarus. You are his friend, he would weep for you. Poor Gabriel in James Joyce's story, tears thickened in his eyes when the thought of the generosity of a love that could end in a death willingly given for his beloved. Weeping because he could not feel it himself. So he lost his identity. Is our identity any clearer – faced by friendship like this? He died to redeem our loveless life, to disclose a peace that can restore us to friendship with God. "Love to the loveless shown that they might lovely be." Another thing he said, almost with his dying breath, addressed not to man but to God, "Father forgive them, they do not know what they are doing." So this is the way that love is to be expressed by Him to the Father, by the Father to us, His forgiveness. That is the expression of love, the creative reason for His death. "He died that we might be forgiven." To establish a principle of love, seen in forgiveness as the ultimate activity of love in a sinful world. Something on which we could build a new life, His life in us, and through us, a new world.

To acknowledge your sin and the separation, guilt and fear that goes with it, to say "I have sinned, I am sorry, forgive me, help me to start again," is to recognise that his life was lived for you, and to claim his forgiveness is to know freedom, reconciliation, and the liberty of love.

Claiming that forgiveness for yourself can be a turning point in your life, turn it upside down – to see everything including your own life from the point of view of His Cross, and through the eyes of God.

Paul describing that experience said, "I have been crucified with Christ and yet I live. Yet not I but Christ lives in me, and the life I now live in the flesh I live by faith in the Son of God who loved me, and gave his life for me. Charles Wesley said, " 'Tis love, 'tis love, thou diedst for me."

The Blood of Jesus

"The blood is the life" says the book of Leviticus. Jesus knew all about that. The Jews worshipped God by killing animals, collecting the blood in great bowls and offering it to God for the sins of the people. An offering of life. They were still doing it in Jesus' day, so when John the Baptist pointed to him and said, "Behold this is the Lamb of God who takes away the sins of the world," it was, you might say, a coded way of telling Jesus just how he would die, and why. There is a thick river of blood that flows through the Bible, as there is also all that red wine, all those grapes, those vines, those cups. All these images converge in the upper room. There are more words of Jesus about his death. "This is my blood which is given for you, do this in remembrance of me." And so it is, and so we do, day by day, repeating the same words, "Lamb of God that takest away the sins of the world, have mercy on us," offering our bowls of wine but repeating "The Blood of Christ" – which brings us to our last reflection.

The Death of Death

John Donne, the Dean of St Paul's, who before he died put his effigy in St Paul's in a funeral shroud, wrote:

> One short sleepe past, wee wake eternally,
> And death shall be no more; death, thou shalt die.

And that is it. "Death shall have no dominion." If Jesus died to share our death, He also died so that we might share His life. There is no fear in death, perfect love casts out fear: and in His perfect love death could not hold Him. Only three days, and He was seen alive, again and again. After forty days He was seen no more, no more localised that is. Jesus, one with the Father, shares His life with us all, as we can share our life with Him. That is the personal story of every Christian who claims the friendship and forgiveness of Jesus on the Cross. Eternal life. "Jesus lives, henceforth is death but the gate of life immortal." As to our sin, well what He offered in blood on earth He offers in love in Heaven. The writer of *The Epistle to the Hebrews* says, "He ever lives to make intercession for us." So it is, and so He does. And as we pray that we may evermore dwell in Him and He in us, so we also proclaim aloud, "Christ has died, Christ is risen, Christ will come again."

Bereavement

COMING TO TERMS WITH LOSS

Address to the Diocesan Clergy Wives,
Bishop Woodward House. Ely 1987

For Christians Easter is central to our understanding of human life on earth, or even living existence on earth. For surely there is a true sense in which the whole of creation plays its part and has its share in the miracle of resurrection. It is no accident that the resurrection is recalled "*In the Spring-time of the Year*", to quote the title of Susan Hill's moving novel about bereavement. Some time ago I was taking part in a conference at Windsor and staying with Stephen Verney, at that time a canon of St George's. It was a time of pain and anxiety for him: his wife was dying of cancer – a lovely person whom I had known well ever since she married Stephen many years ago. He gave the conference some moving and inspiring bible studies filled with a vision of the Spirit. When he took me to my room he said, "Susan Hill wrote her last novel in this room." So, for a few days we seemed to move between the painful reality of approaching death, the assurance of the power and comfort of God, and the mysterious way in which we pass on the experience of living, and dying, and living again – which is so much a part of Susan Hill's books. And of course not of hers alone, but of other writers. Many of you will know the little book by C. S. Lewis in which he records the death of his wife, and his grappling with God, A *Grief Observed*.

The poets in particular have tried to speak for us. So Henry Vaughan says:

They are all gone into the world of light.
And I alone sit lingering here;

Their very memory is fair and bright
And my sad thoughts doth clear.

I see them walking in an air of glory
Whose light doth trample on my days:
My days, which are at best but dull and hoary
Mere glimmering and decays.

Dear beauteous Death, the jewel of the Just
Shining nowhere but in the dark;
What mysteries do lie beyond thy dust
Could man outlook that mark.

But is death so "beauteous", as he says? Surely it is often
violent, cruel, sudden, apparently meaningless, unexpected, an expression of inhumanity so overwhelming as
to defy description and only leave us numb. The ferry
disaster, the pitiful picture of a little boy unable to comprehend, and the need of so many people to make him a
symbol of their loss; the harrowed face of the wife of PC
Blakelock, a picture that haunts me still, grappling with
grief, the fear, the aggression and bewilderment of a
whole community of people caught in a tragedy that
encompassed the police, the black people, the simple,
onfused and frightened families faced with a violence that
erupted all around them, out of control. He was a "bobby
on the beat", a community policeman, someone who cared
and was known to care. When he died a violent death
something in the whole community died – trust, confidence, loyalty, and fear bred fear against a background of
bereavement.

In recent years the word has been used more widely as if
to acknowledge that death is a part of living. A man is
forced to retire from a job he has done for many years and
in which he has been wholly and happily absorbed – his
loss is a bereavement. A loved teacher leaves a school – the
school is bereaved, and so on.

But against that background, bereavement means for

most of us something infinitely personal; so personal that though Christians have, in theory, resources with which to cope with it that are denied to others, it is not always the case that they feel able to fall back on the strength which Grace supplies. The reality for us is that we do not live between the polarities of life and death, the Crib and the Cross, as the world does; but between Conception and Resurrection, the great mysteries of our faith. What was conceived in the womb of Mary was Jesus, the Son of God who gives us the first intimation of eternity, of immortality. So every mother, wife, every woman who has ever borne a child, every aunt who has ever suffered vicariously for a beloved nephew or niece, every sister who has grieved over a lost brother, carries within herself the capability of being conscious, (humanly, physically speaking), of the bearing into the world of Eternal Being.

In Jesus we see God identified with all humanity, every single human, living creature, all of them for ever. He is the little boy who lost his parents and grandparents in the ferry disaster, and His grief grows in that lad's uncomprehending eyes. A human disaster and loss too large for him to truly understand as yet, is not too large for the Son of God, who is also the Son of Mankind. That is at one end of the theological spectrum, and it finds its focus not only in the birth and life of Jesus – which is clearly understandable in human terms – but supremely in His death.

Once again, it would be reasonable to infer that it is His mother, and through her all women, who enters into the significance of it so far as His actual anguish is concerned. Jacopone da Todi, the Franciscan poet, expressed this so well in the familiar hymn, *Stabat Mater*:

At the Cross her station keeping
Stood the mournful mother weeping
Close to Jesus at the last.
Through her soul, of joy bereavèd

Bowed with anguish, deeply grievèd
Now at length the sword hath passed.

Perhaps the most telling example of the identification of
God with the past of man in this century is to be found in
the horror of the Holocaust, the determined extermination
of six million Jews by Hitler. Edwin Robertson writing in
Theology says, "In Germany in the Thirties, the Jew, Jesus of
Nazareth, would have been humiliated and eventually dis-
patched in a gas chamber by believing Christians." And it
is no less telling to recall that He dies daily in the arms of
His dying mother in the thousands of babies in famine-
stricken Ethiopia or war-wrecked Mozambique.

That however is not the full extent of the mystery. If we
are committed to knowing God in the mystery of
Conception we are also committed to knowing God in the
mystery of Resurrection. Some people have as much difficulty with the one as with the other. It is so clearly not just
this life going on for ever and ever; though there is something about this life which has continuity, something which
has to do with recognition, with knowing, something
which has at last become clear, in fact which seemed to
need death in order to become clear.

What is that, you might ask? Is it not that we share, from
the beginning, that is from *our* conception, in the immortality of God, something which not only binds us to Him
but also to one another in Him. It might be that humanly
speaking we are particularly bound to the mother who
bore us, but we are no less bound by our common human
nature, the humanity with which He made himself part of
the common stock. At the same time we share that eternal
destiny which He came to demonstrate. It is always there,
often remarkably evident in the innocence of childhood,
even if confused with a heightened capacity for deception
or sometimes just drowned in the depravity and sadness,
the deprivations of the world. Hidden by the hard shell of
our all too human being, it can shine out in chosen souls or

chosen circumstances. Heroism, unselfishness, just plain human love can have about it hints of that unquenchable eternity and immortality all of which is part of continuing daily life. Then in old or older age this quality of immortality which is so subtle and difficult to define can glow in lives like a sort of glory and radiate a reality that defies and denies the diminishments of age and frailty, indeed it is sometimes the very fragility of our human lives which appears to release it. We call it grace or holiness. Sometimes it is the prolonged suffering which goes before death which becomes the refining means of revealing it.

By my bed I have a small crucifix which was left me in her will by a girl I first met when we were both patients in our twenties in Papworth sanatorium. We were seriously ill. She had a great deal of rather brutal surgery which was the best that could be done at that time. After a year or so I recovered well enough to become a Franciscan and eventually led a very active life which for many years included travelling all over the world. She remained a patient for another forty years and died in the same place. Yet for all her inactivity they were years of remarkable fulfilment, a radiant hope and increasing creative love. She contained in herself such a certainty of life that she became more and more a source of strength to others. It was not just that she prayed, though she certainly did, but that she had a power of *being* that seemed an inexhaustible resource for all those who came to see her. Her death was a triumph, the final liberation of her love and though we were bereaved this seemed released to be even more present with us than she was before.

Also in my room, facing me as I write, is an ash tray – these days full of paper clips – all that I have of another friend, the wife of a priest. Lively, vivacious, beautiful, turning every head when she walked into a room, a brilliant talker, and always with something intelligent or witty to say, endlessly extravagantly generous and kind, and a marvellous listener. I stayed with them one summer, ending my holiday with a long slow meal on a warm evening, talking of friends, making plans for the future. The following morning I rang just to say thank you. She said, "I don't feel very well, a bit of a headache". An hour later her husband rang to tell me she had, quite suddenly, died. Once the actual truth of that had inhabited me (and I can feel it now as I did then) it seemed as if some part of me had died also. Her capacity for friendship at the deepest level was quite remarkable and when, as was soon the case, we shared our grief it was only to discover that everyone thought he or she was the "best" friend, the closest, as near to her as her husband or her daughter. That friendship which was too unique, too much a source of love to be taken for granted, has always been with us, part I believe of her immortality because it sprang from her friendship with God which for her was even more real. That was all twenty years ago, yet when the same friends meet – diminished now a little in number – we know she could not be replaced because she is, in so many ways, very much alive to us.

What I think I am trying to suggest is that bereavement is an inevitable and unavoidable passageway in life. Death is a matter of a moment – as you might turn a corner and be almost as near yet out of sight, or walk from one room to another yet be in the same house, or on the same floor. Death is the unique experience which will be common to us all, the one thing we all have for certain in common. Isn't it strange how much of the planning in this world, much of our own planning, is done against a background of suspended belief in our mortality, as if we had all the time in the world?

I was preparing an address recently for the hundredth anniversary of a church when it suddenly came into my mind that in a little over a hundred years from now every single person alive on the surface of the world at this present time will be dead. So death is a single personal experience. Not so bereavement. We are left with the consciousness of

loss: and it is the source of our mourning. It should also be
a totally expected element in life to be suffered and shared
by us all. That it is a common experience in no way makes
it less personal. A mother bearing the loss of a son or
daughter has something in common with countless
mothers, but nothing can take the place of that special relationship of love. Perhaps even more acutely is felt the death
of a husband or wife. If in a marriage of any length there
has been that growing together which makes one flesh of a
marriage then for one to die is, for the time being, for two
to die. Neither of these are direct experiences for me so I
know of them only in the shared life of my friends.

The experience of bereavement came to me early in life –
as to so many of my generation. Almost all the men I loved
most, and one in particular, died suddenly, killed in the
Second World War. I learnt how impossible it was to say
anything adequate to their mothers, discovered that eventually I could be loved a little for their sake but never in
their place. I watched my father die slowly after several
operations, and as by then I had just become a priest,
administered the only sacraments he ever received at my
hands. I remember feeling closer to him and my family
than I had ever been, and bereavement being a drawing
together in love, something that has always remained and
was given even greater intensity when my mother died
three years ago. Strange that at ninety-eight this had an
inevitability about it that still could not save me thinking of
her as immortal. Like St Francis she really could and did
say "Welcome Sister Death", and her vitality, her profound
sense of being, the enthusiasm with which she had always
embraced life, not only for herself, but wholly and
unselfishly for others, combined with a Scottish realism
that included an absolute conviction of the power of prayer
and the communion of saints left little room for a wrong
approach to death. She prepared herself for that, she also
prepared us to be left in the other room, and made a party

of it, a shared experience that welcomed her back in another way.

In spite of that, it took me a long time to adjust to a different pattern in life. I didn't know it, and could resent violently the well meaning efforts of my friends and brothers to, as they say, "help me through" my bereavement. In retrospect I know the feelings were related to other symptoms of bereavement I had experienced on three or four other occasions in my life. The rational part of me, the part that knows the answers for other people, just cannot apply reason to my case. Some people, though in their heart of hearts they know it doesn't make sense, take out their resentment on God. I don't feel that, but then I don't feel anything except an appalling soul-destroying despair, a cold clamp of steel, and dull ache as if nothing could ever again be the same. I can be glad, truly glad, that for the person concerned there will be no more pain, cancer, stroke, cruel discomfort, or slow erosion of life – "but", I say, *"what about me?"* I too have been paralysed, some part of me has also died. And I think that is true. When my friend Sam died suddenly in America of a heart attack it seemed for months that I could not live with any comfort again in a world without him. I tried to be a strength for his wife, his children – we had always been very close – but for a while I could not speak of him without wanting spontaneously to weep. It took a long time to discover how much alive he is, not only in his writing but in his students. I see the smirch of his smile, hear echoes of his voice. I find the gentle modulation of his reasoning in so much of my world. The Atlantic is no longer a barrier.

So it took time. It took also the association of those who seemed to know that his death would seem something more to me, and didn't try to offer substitutes. Patient waiting, loving, caring. Not using those words which can so easily discount comfort. If bereavement is the dark tunnel to life then by all means take my hand as we go through – but don't pull me, or even squeeze me. Help me to keep walking but don't please, don't keep whispering instruction in my ear. It may not help me to hug my grief, but sometimes it is all I have got. It's a paradox, but I need to be alone, yet I am afraid of being lonely – yet if you try to comfort me I shall shrink to the point of screaming. I've seen people cross the road because they don't know what they would say if they met me face to face. Bereavement can be like an illness. Other people cross the road in order to meet me face to face and tell me how to cope. I'm not sure which is worse.

A young woman whose husband died recently told me how some of her friends got together to make sure she was never alone; inviting her to dinner parties, finding sympathetic men to be her partner. It was all so kind, and so hopeless. "As if", she said, "anything could take the place of John." So she retreated either to tears, to emptiness, to frenzied activity, or to her children. They too had their bereavement. Four teenagers from fifteen to twenty, four separate and distinct griefs and none of them quite like hers. Neither was the death of the father, an anticipated death from cancer, very much like the death, rather more suddenly, of their grandmother, their only other experience of someone dying who was, as is sometimes the case with grannies, in a sense even closer to them. To make her bereavement a projection of theirs finally proved an impossibility and in the end it seemed to those of us who stood by to share when we could, that it was they who found the strength to help her. Finally, after many months, she knew she needed, and accepted, the help which would lead her into her new, her present life. Her experience has been reproduced, of course, countless times, yet it cannot be repeated too often that it is also totally and completely hers.

Eastertide is, as I said near the beginning, a time when we are faced with the classical examples of bereavement in the Christian experience. For Jesus "the strife was o'er, the battle done". How often have I felt an echo of those words

217

when I have watched the peace of death fall finally across a face which has suffered long and painful illnesses. How, sometimes I have really longed for it to be over for them. But for the disciples, it was the beginning, the beginning of bereavement. Each of them coping in his own way. Peter and John tried to bury their grief by going back to the nets. A new life, a life without Jesus now to be lived – so they returned to what they knew. With the women it was different. Their consolation was to go to the tomb to weep, to do what they could for his body, to be busy in another way.

To them all Jesus came in another way, at the tomb, by the sea, on the road. What we have in the gospel stories is their recorded experience. Written down some years afterwards perhaps, and no doubt coloured by subsequent events, indeed having a formality which sprang from constant telling and retelling. None of that detracts, I think, from the central event. Jesus came to them. Whatever you call it, however you describe it, Jesus insists by his presence that there is a continuity beyond the physical death of our bodies. I cannot force or oblige anyone to believe this. Indeed it is such a precious, intimate truth that I would not want to argue about it with those who regard it as fiction or fancy lacking scientific proof. Yet because it was true for Jesus, so I believe it is true for everyone who dies. Not an exceptional thing, not something that requires special faith, or any faith at all. I mean I believe it is true whether other people believe it or not.

It should come as no surprise therefore if from time to time we become aware of the closeness of the dead to us. To explain how I know this would be difficult, not because it is difficult, but because it is very easy to mislead. I'm not talking about ghosts, or spirits, I'm not specially psychic and I discourage the use of mediums.

Indeed my only reason for speaking of this very important part of our experience is that I really believe it to be of significant help in bereavement. Not perhaps immediately, but as time passes, then the awareness can grow that someone we love and of whom we have felt a part, who dies, opens as it were a window on another part of that world of the Spirit to which we both belong. "Don't forget", they say, "we are still one, this world is yours as well as mine." Charles Wesley says in a familiar hymn:

> Let saints on earth in concert sing
> With those whose work is done
> For all the servants of our King
> In heaven and earth are one.

So the departed can reach out to minister to us, and in prayer we can feel a real, almost tangible, presence with us. This too cannot be forced, and for some people at some time it could be a pretty poor consolation. So there is a time for everything, and time too is in the hands of God.

> The life of Grace and Glory is the same.
> The life of Grace is, by another name
>   Heaven on earth:
> And death is but a change in range
>   And nothing strange.

Retreat Addresses

ON THE SECOND LETTER
TO TIMOTHY

*Lambeth Palace, Retreat for Primates prior to
Lambeth Conference. July 1988*

2 TIMOTHY 1:1-10

From Paul, apostle of Jesus Christ by the will of God, whose promise of life is fulfilled in Christ Jesus, to Timothy his dear son.

Grace, mercy, and peace to you from God the Father and our Lord Jesus Christ.

I thank God – whom I, like my forefathers, worship with a pure intention – when I mention you in my prayers; this I do constantly night and day. And when I remember the tears you shed, I long to see you again to make my happiness complete. I am reminded of the sincerity of your faith, a faith which was alive in Lois your grandmother and Eunice your mother before you, and which, I am confident, lives in you also.

That is why I now remind you to stir into flame the gift of God which is within you through the laying on of my hands. For the spirit that God gave us is no craven sprit, but one to inspire strength, love, and self-discipline. So never be ashamed of your testimony to our Lord, nor of me his prisoner, but take your share of suffering for the sake of the Gospel, in the strength that comes from God. It is he who brought us salvation and called us to a dedicated life not for any merit of ours but of his own purpose and his own grace, which was granted to us in Christ Jesus from all eternity, but has now at length been brought fully into view by the appearance on earth of our Saviour Jesus Christ. For he has broken the power of death and brought life and immortality to light through the Gospel. [NEB]. ·

A few weeks ago I was visiting our Franciscan Brothers in Belfast; switching on the radio to get news of European football I heard instead a news flash announcing the sudden, violent death of six English soldiers, blown up by a bomb planted on their truck. It was in Lisburn, and the following morning I was there attending the Diocesan Synod, the first of the newly appointed Bishop of Connor. Hanging over it was the horror of this event and for the Bishop the need to be seen as the Pastor, leader, centre of prayer and compassion. The same day I talked with Bishop Cahal Daly, the Roman Catholic – a man of rare goodness and love, whose eyes spoke eloquently of the pain he shared in the face of this senseless slaughter. Both men, as I observed them, united by the eloquence of penitence, of forgiveness, compassion and reconciliation. So suffering made them one in Christ - and He in them. Well, that sort of incident is being repeated in one way or another in all the countries from which we have come here. The political, social, ecumenical, doctrinal, racial elements in it are reflected in all the main issues to be discussed in this conference. There are no easy answers – in some cases apparently no immediate answer at all. The only consolation and strength for the Christians – and non-Christians – lies in those two men from whom, in such a moment of crisis, something particular is expected. You know the feeling. In retrospect you may be praised for your political statement - but you will be loved and remembered for the pain in your eyes and your prayers.

For a short while we have an opportunity to enter into silence and make our response to the God and Father of us all who waits for us. It would be good if for just this time we could put resolutely aside all such weighty matters, for which there has been so much preparation, and let God

speak to us of His love and His calling to each one of us. A
short time, using an old phrase "to make our souls" and
wait on our Father.

Returning from Jerusalem. I was going down the escala-
tor at Heathrow. In front of me was a devout Jewish family. Father and sons in broad brimmed black hats, long
coats, ringlets. The smallest son ran on ahead adventur-
ously down the steps till he got near the bottom and was
then suddenly fearful how to get off! Looking back he
cried, "Abba, Abba!" Strange how the scriptures come to
life. So, Paul says, God sent His son in order that we might
attain the status of sons and to prove it he has sent the
Spirit of His Son in our heart crying "Abba, Father". He
also adds, "Now that you have acknowledged God - rather
than he has acknowledged you - how can you turn back?"
Well, we probably don't want to, but a mitre in no way
diminishes our status as sons, and our confidence and hope
lie in the awareness that He has acknowledged us. "Now
are we the sons of God – we shall be like Him, we shall see
Him as He is." At the recent memorial service for Michael
Ramsey it was so clear from all the readings from his
works, from everyone who spoke, that here was a man who
held together in himself both a profound sense of the
Fatherhood of God, a simple and absolute acceptance of his
own sonship as a child, and at the same time an equally
profound awareness of the vision, the majesty, the glory -
the wonder of eternity and a consciousness that we do well
to acknowledge both the dignity, and yet the "long littleness of life".

With thoughts such as this in mind I would like to base
these talks on some words from the Second Epistle of St
Paul to Timothy. It puts us in perspective. In the New
English Bible, the Second Epistle to Timothy is headed
"The character of a Christian minister". It seems widely
agreed that though this letter contains much Pauline
thought, even some extracts of his writing, it is probably
not written by him. Then by whom?

The man to whom, under God, I owe my vocation, indeed, my life in Christ, died nearly thirty years ago. He was Algy Robertson, the Minister of the Franciscans. A little man with an astounding and powerful personality, a brilliant preacher, teacher, evangelist and man of God. He had an infinite capacity for making friends of all ages who loved him with almost exaggerated affection. They knew each other, treasured his sermons, his endless, almost indecipherable, letters, told many stories about him. Soon after we met I became his secretary, travelled everywhere with him, and like so many others thought him my most intimate friend. I knew all his ways. He was untidy, unpunctual, slept little, prayed much, and died long before he should from taking no care of his body. I little realised that one day I would be Minister in his place.

A clever writer could have collected all that information, anecdotes, personal recollections and written an imaginary letter from Algy to Michael. A final letter of instruction, warning and admonition before he died.

"Two Timothy" is just such a brilliant literary device. An imaginary letter from prison, made plausible by the mention of many friends, but very serious in its intention – and as relevant for us the successors of Timothy as it was when it was written.

The dramatic setting is the last days of St Paul's life in a Roman prison – the last letter, the swan song, of a man condemned to death, who has already survived one long trial and escaped the lions [4:16-18]. Paul's ideas, even extracts from his remembered words mean that the whole letter has the urgency of crisis, the pathos of personal parting and the passion of personal conviction.

The Church itself was already emerging with a certain structural ministry. In 1 Timothy 3 we read: "To aspire to leadership is an honourable ambition. Our leader, therefore, or bishop, must be above reproach, faithful to his one wife, sober, temperate, courteous, a good teacher" and so on, reminding us rather of a Vacancy in See Committee.

More importantly, there is a strong sense of urgency. He is conscious of the Great Day [1:12,18] "I charge you solemnly", he says, "by his coming and appearance and his reign" [4:1] "You must face the fact", he demands, "the final age of this world will be a time of troubles" [3:1] and then goes on to describe not only his world, but surely ours as well - giving this letter a timelessness which makes it something for me, something for now [2 Tim. 3:1 -7].

It was written to warn Timothy to stand firm in the face of a major heresy and the infection of a false teaching that will spread, he says, like gangrene. Well, it could be written for any one of us.

But first we are reminded of the priority of God in our own personal lives, and that gives us some thoughts for our prayers tonight. "It is he who brought us to salvation and called us to a dedicated life, not for any merit of ours, but of his own purpose and his own grace, which was granted us in Christ Jesus from all eternity" [2 Tim. 1:9]. In the King James Bible it reads more directly, "who hath saved us, and called us with a holy calling not according to our works, but according to his own purpose and grace, which was given us in Christ Jesus before the world began." We are confronted with God, who saved us, called us, gave us the grace of Jesus Himself, and all this, for each one of us personally, uniquely, as part of the purpose of God from all eternity.

I have been seized of late of this wonder that in every individual person I meet there is the the image of God, distorted, defaced, dented, perhaps, almost beyond recognition, but there. In Jesus alone has the glory of man been revealed entirely – "we beheld his glory, the glory as of the only begotten of the Father, full of grace and truth." And because it is in Him, it is, somewhere, in us. In the oppressors as well as the oppressed – in the IRA bombers as well as the young soldiers blown up and burned by them. The gift of God, through Christ Jesus, is the full restoration of

His image in each one of us. "We shall be like him," says St John, "we shall see Him as he is." That was always His purpose, His longing, nothing in the world matters more to God, and to me. To long for this, to live for this, is not selfish or self-centred or ambitious. It is a longing reflected in the lives of all His saints. Do you recall the language of Augustine in *The Confessions?*

> Too late have I loved you, Beauty so old and so new! I have learned to love you too late. You were within me, and I looked out into the world where I sought you outside myself, and in my deformity searched for you there, and ran after the beauties you have made. You were with me, but I was not with you. . . . You called and shouted, and broke into my deafness. You flashed and shone, and dispelled my blindness. . . . You touched me, and I burnt for your peace.

So, says St Paul, "It is He who brought us to salvation," and called with a holy calling. We are reminded of our conversion and our vocation.

Of St Paul's conversion on the Damascus road we know only too well, when God flashed and shone. The time, the place, and the violent intervention of God in his life was never to be forgotten by him. And that is true of countless others, perhaps of some of us here. By contrast St Paul in this letter is reminding Timothy of what is frequently the more usual path of conversion. Paul knew the family of Timothy, they all met at Listra on one of his missionary journeys. Now he reminds him of the faith he was given by his mother and grandmother. He says, "from a child you have known the sacred scriptures that are able to make you wise with salvation which is in Christ Jesus" [2 Tim. 3:15]. Perhaps more than that there was the loving friendship of Paul himself. A friendship of such depth that it is remembered with tears and longing [1:3]. Timothy is in every way

225

a son in the Lord – one to whom you give your best, and from whom you look for the best.

May I suggest that we might begin this time of silence by looking back in gratitude to God who brought us to salvation. Consider your conversion to Christ, the men and women, the events, the opportunities, the choices that made it, that are still making it possible. In this we are united, in this we speak as one, that we have all experienced and continue to experience the converting power of the love of God in our lives. We, who are being changed from glory to glory, who are being brought into the fullest realisation of our sonship. And this, above all things, gives the character and quality to all we say and do, as we think and speak, unconsciously respond to that continuing experience.

And however we begin it leads always to the vision of God, God's prior action. For Moses a small bush burns, for Isaiah the house of God glows with glory. John just looks at Jesus and follows him, Peter is plunged in tears to find a salvation in forgiveness. John of the Cross and John Bunyan had this in common, they found Christ in prison – and for all there is the testimony of Paul.

> I have been crucified with Christ yet I live. Yet not I but Christ liveth in me, and the life that I now live I live by faith in the Son of God who loved me and gave himself for me. *Gal 2:20*

Conversion springs from the vision of God, our personal salvation through the Cross of Christ. The Methodists have rightly been celebrating the conversion of John Wesley – who certainly knew the date and place when his heart was strangely warmed, and he accepted Christ as his personal saviour. In the words of his brother Charles, " 'Tis love, 'tis love, thou diedst for me, I hear thy whisper in my heart." Could there be apparently a more dissimilar person to these brothers than John Henry Newman? Yet he made his motto in life, "Heart speaks to heart." It is no fancy that at the heart of the matter is our total surrender to His love. "Herein is love, not that we loved God, but that He first loved us," as we surrender our lives – again and again – to his love, as love responds to love, so we discover a wholeness in our lives we never knew before. We find something in ourselves that can respond in compassion to the divided world, a world for ever searching and longing for its lost self. If we live in Him, and He in us, then we see the world through His eyes, the eyes of His eternal purpose. "So *that's* what He meant it to be, that is the goal." How different from the way the world planned it.

It is against that background we can see the full consequences of this calling. "It is He who brought us to salvation and called us with a holy calling." Called to be Christ, called also with the particular responsibilities of our priesthood. Later in this letter the writer speaks of vessels of value, set aside for his Master's use [2:21]. We are here not in the first place of our own choice, though we were free to respond to Him, not for any merit of ours, but of His own purpose and His own grace. The wonder of it. If we are amazed it could be so, surely there is also reassurance. For many of us this Lambeth will be the last. Already the biographies and autobiographies are being written. But can any one say what really happened when you first knew you would be a priest, let alone a bishop or archbishop. God alone knows that cannot be written – but hard, perhaps painful as it is, to recapture that first leap of directed love in surrender to God's plan is to fall into the eternal purpose, be renewed with his eternal grace and power. "Stir up the Spirit that is in you, by the laying on of my hand" [1:6,7]. The Spirit of strength, love, and self discipline.

There is a passage from 2 Corinthians 6 which I have quoted so often in my Society that one of the sisters wrote it out and framed it, then gave it to me and said, "There you are, stick it up in your room." Because I often feel a fraud, because I feel I have failed, because I know I don't practise what I preach, and am not the person I present to the world, or that people think I am but – because the best part of me wants to be true to my salvation and my calling, I take comfort in these words:

> We are the impostors who speak the truth, the unknown men whom all men know, dying we still live on, disciplined by suffering we are not done to death, in sorrow we have always cause for joy; poor ourselves we bring wealth to many, penniless we own the world.
>
> *2 Cor 6:8-10 [NEB]*

Take your share of hardship, like a good soldier of Christ Jesus. A soldier on active service will not let himself be involved in civilian affairs; he must be wholly at his commanding officer's disposal. Again, no athlete can win a prize unless he has kept the rules. The farmer who gives his labour has first claim on the crop. Reflect on what I say, for the Lord will help you to full understanding.

Remember Jesus Christ, risen from the dead, born of David's line. This is the theme of my gospel, in whose service I am exposed to hardship, even to the point of being shut up like a common criminal; but the word of God is not shut up. And I endure it all for the sake of God's chosen ones, with this end in view, that they too may attain the glorious and eternal salvation which is in Christ Jesus. [NEB]

The inspired author of this letter from Paul to Timothy has made it very personal and challenging with, sometimes, almost a sense of rebuke, as if Timothy were falling short of the high vocation to which he had been called by God. It is that challenge which makes it of particular value to all those who share that ministry. Ours is a service for the Church which shares the very life and service of Christ – "living", as Paul says, "by the faith and love which are ours in Christ Jesus" [1:13].

And our service is the proclamation of the Gospel [4:5] of which we are to be heralds, apostles, teachers [1:11] that through the Gospel, life and immortality and light have been brought into the world. To that end we must be prepared to take our share of suffering, of hardship, for the sake of the Gospel.

This idea of sharing the suffering of Christ occurs several times. It is here in 2:3, "take your share of hardship like a good soldier of Christ Jesus", in 1:8 as we have already seen, in 2:9, "I am exposed to hardship", and in 4:5, "face hardship, work to spread the Gospel".

We know how literally true this has been for some of our brethren in recent years as in the past, in Uganda, in Latin America, in Asia.

One of my privileges as Minister General of a world-wide brotherhood is to have this truth of the life of the Church brought vividly into my own life. It is one thing to read of the death of Vivian Redlynch in England – another thing altogether, to stand on the beach in New Guinea where he awaited the coming of the Japanese forces and gave his life in defence of the Gospel. Or when I watch my Solomon Island brothers re-enacting the death of Coleridge Pattesson, his body floating in a canoe with five wounds in it and a palm branch with five knots.

Paul knew that to say, "I am crucified with Christ", meant to share the glory of the Cross - but also the pain, and is not afraid again and again, to point to his own suffering for the Gospel: imprisonment, beating, stoning, rejection, threats as evidence. Is there any reason to suppose that things have changed; is such suffering reserved only for the few, the exceptional, those caught in the crossfire of a divided and hostile world?

Confronted with this, Paul points to the quality in human life and Christian experience of *endurance*. In 2:10 "I endure it all for the elect's sake - God's chosen ones", and in 2:12, "If we endure we shall reign with him." In 3:11 he speaks of "all the persecutions I endured". To follow him in that is to follow "Jesus who for the joy that lay ahead of him endured the cross, making light of its disgrace and has taken his seat at the right hand of the throne of God." So may we consider for a moment the place of endurance in our lives.

John Whale in his book the *"Future of Anglicanism"* published by Mowbrays in preparation for this Lambeth Conference, has some rather deflating things to say about future bishops. He says firmly that they will be chosen not for their churchmanship, but their wide tolerance – which could sound a slightly barbed remark. Secondly, he says:

> Bishops will not be loved. They are in any case likely to be without the loyalty accorded on grounds of churchmanship. More than that, though, the qualities that make good managers are not loveable. Managers may themselves love their charges but they must not expect to be loved by them. You cannot oblige people to do what they are reluctant to do, or to stop doing what they enjoy doing and expect to retain their active affection. Perhaps Bishops have never been as well loved as the memorial tablets claim. It is noticeable that beloved Bishops, like miracles, are always in the past. Either way their chance of being beloved in the future is dwindling.

Well, let's hope he is no more prophetic in that part of the book than he seems to be in other parts of it!

Endurance in the face of hostility: There is no doubt, however, that from time to time we have to face real hostility not only from outside, but inside the Church. The sort of media madness that pounces on every pronouncement, determined to find a point of conflict or scandal, because that, and not the truth, is the selling point, can be deeply divisive. The apparently deliberate distortions turn the knife in a wound which is already real enough. There is always pain when the household of God disagrees – indeed our divided Churches is both our biggest scandal and the source of our greatest pain. Ignorance and hostility make it infinitely worse. A certain degree of prominence makes us an easy and obvious target, and no matter how carefully we choose our words we can get it wrong, or be made to seem wrong. Verbal violence can be the source of very real mental and physical pain.

To persist and endure in the face of apathy and indifference or ignorance: To retain a cutting edge in the face of the enemies which lie as often within the Church as outside it. We can, after all, say of the hostile political or secular voices, that they can't hear what we say, or the way we say it – they belong to another world. But the argument is less convincing when the contradiction comes from within our own family. There is a sort of apathy which it is hard to fight against, entrenched positions which remain unchanged in spite of our best endeavours. It requires real endurance to work away, by argument, example, prayer, patience and long-suffering, at what can seem like the almost subversive attitudes of our own colleagues, and remain positive, creative, and constructive as well.

To endure in the face of our own weaknesses: I do not mean our sins, but the frequent awareness that I am just the person I am. Impetuous – too quick on the draw with speech or judgement, or too hesitant, so anxious to see every side of the case that I appear waffley, vague, "lacking in leadership". To endure in the face of actual physical weaknesses – I personally envy the people who only seem to need four hours sleep, when I can't manage unless I have much more. Paul had one thorn in his flesh, while I have a whole bush of them! Anxiety about eyesight, arthritis, or any one or more of the inevitable physical consequences of advancing years. To endure in fighting the temptation of becoming the authoritarian figure who has an answer for everything – or to assume a fake modesty that has no answer at all. To endure in the face of loneliness, or the fear of not being loved, or the hard fact that, as with everyone, we shall not escape the loss of friends or the crumbling sometimes of relationships, of strains within our own lives that affect even those that are closest.

To endure in the face of our sins: We, more than most, will know that we are called not so much to be a prince, but a penitent, a penitent among the people of God. We are called to pray with Jesus, "Father, forgive them, they do not know what they are doing", and that remains true in all those places in the world from which we come. From a privileged position we can sometimes see that more clearly than anyone else; not merely that something is socially or politically wrong, morally irresponsible or profoundly selfish, but an actual denial of God's own purpose and grace, the very deeds which crucify Christ afresh, and put him to a perpetual shame. To be close enough to Jesus to see the world as he sees it, mankind through his eyes, the denial of love through his heart – to register the shame, the pain, the sense of outrage, the violence to all he intends for me, commits us also to being his voice which declares the sin, and the channel which makes known the forgiveness. To be, above all, the means of reconciliation at all sorts of levels in life.

But if this is to be a constant factor in our lives and witness, then it will only be true and effective before God (the world will not necessarily ever understand completely) if we are ourselves constantly aware of the need to live close to that same forgiving love in our own lives.

When Jesus says, "Father forgive them", He is speaking for all mankind, and for each and every man and woman individually. In the heart of God the Father we are each of us identified absolutely for the person we are, exposed to the occupational hazards of our vocation, some of them all the more dangerous because it would be supposed that we of all men would be free of them or the temptations that go with them. Pride or Envy, Sloth – or that "sickness unto death" as Kierkegaard called it – Despair. Arrogance or Conceit – our failures in love, because we demanded too much from others, or too little; failed to recognise the selfishness of what we asked from them, or the physical and mental indulgence involved. Paul says, "Turn from the wayward impulses of youth" – the King James Bible puts it more simply "flee youthful lusts" – particularly those, perhaps that chase after us into old age.

Sin is a great equaliser. To be truly penitent among the people of God, and for the people of God, is to be perpetually renewed in the power of forgiveness. And forgiveness, a true and profound forgiveness that springs from the

233

Cross, from the very voice of God himself, is the most liberating and reconciling power in the world.

Francis of Assisi sang in his *Canticle of the Creatures*, "Praised be my Lord by those who pardon one another for his love's sake, for thou O Most Mighty shall give them a crown." And Paul in this letter says, "l endure it all for the sake of God's chosen ones that they may attain the glorious and eternal salvation which is in Christ Jesus" [2:10]. "If we endure we shall reign with him."

The monotonous thing about my own confessions is that they seem to have changed very little since I first started making them, about sixty years ago. The glorious thing about them is that I am assured again and again of the full forgiveness won by Christ for me, once and for all on the Cross.

Perhaps it is that, as we are assured of forgiveness, we know with a certainty that can never be diminished, that we have been with Jesus. That is the base line of our common witness – that we have "been with Jesus". It can't be acted out or assumed. If it is there it will be recognised and we will be known as partners with God in His Kingdom and of His Christ; and we can say, in the company of the forgiven, our God reigns.

Above all things forgiveness is a positive affirmation of the Divine Love. The invariably creative contribution we can make in every deadlock or divide. It is no simplistic solution to the human situation. The heroin addict is not miraculously and suddenly cured, the political despot changed, the religious fanatic reconciled on the spot. But the addict, whether to drugs, political power or religious intransigence, discovers the door is no longer locked on the other side. As others once opened a door that enabled us to walk as the sons of God, so we, with this universal key of forgiveness, are called to open the door for others – free the captives, liberate the prisoners of sin and selfishness.

That will indeed demand a personal union with Christ – and endless endurance.

Every inspired scripture has its use for teaching the truth and refuting error or for reformation of manners and discipline in right living, so that the man who belongs to God may be efficient and equipped for good work of every kind.

I noticed earlier how the opening of this Epistle of Paul to Timothy seems to describe so accurately not only the world of his day, but of ours:

Men will love nothing but money and self; they will be arrogant, boastful and abusive, with no respect for parents, no gratitude, no piety, no natural affection; they will be implacable in their hatreds, scandal mongers, intemperate and fierce, strangers to all goodness, traitors, adventurers, swollen with self importance. They will be men who put pleasure in the place of God, men who preserve the outward form of religion, but are a standing denial of its reality. [2 Timothy 3:1-5]

Perhaps it is a bit cynical, but when I look at the "Yuppie" world of this country, at any rate in the South East, that sounds like a fairly accurate assessment of much that I see: and no doubt it is equally true of many of the industrial areas of the world, and those other countries affected by the same values.

The practical advice given by Paul to Timothy as a Church leader faced with such conditions is clear and uncompromising. "You must," he says, "stand by the truths you have learned and are assured of" [3:14]. More than that, he points to himself as an example. "You know," he says, "my teaching, my resolution, faith, patience, spirit of love and my fortitude in the face of persecution."[3:10]. He returns to this warning about persecution which he says will come to all who want to live a godly life.

We live in a world in which political and national sovereignty is related to economic security, and where racial and religious issues are harnessed to these ends in a way which frequently leads to conflict. There is just such a situation on our doorstep in Northern Ireland. We are committed to recognising the voice of God in the Gospel of our Lord Jesus Christ speaking to us out of these conditions. We shall be accused sometimes of declaring too narrow a message, too simple an application of the Word of God; and we shall also be accused, at any rate by those parties who disagree with us, of interfering in politics or being moral hypocrites. There is nothing new in that. Our commitment to Christ and His Church, His people, remains absolute. In 2 Cor 5:14 Paul says, "The love of Christ leaves me no choice." And in 2 Cor 5:17, "When anyone is united to Christ there is a new creation, the old order has gone, a new order has already begun." The continuing problem for us, and one which seems to increase with the passing of time, is the gap in understanding. Speaking and thinking with the liberating power of the Spirit in his new creation, our words, our ideas, our teaching and our truths are misunderstood – sometimes within the household of God, let alone by those outside it.

What we cannot avoid – and wouldn't want to – is the challenge clearly stated here. Like a roll of drums and the sound of trumpets it is put in the inescapable context of our future hope.

Before God, and before Christ Jesus, who is to judge men living and dead, I charge you solemnly by his coming appearance and his reign, proclaim the message, press it home on all occasions, convenient or inconvenient.

The NEB has a marginal note that reads "be on duty at all times" – rather like that . . . face hardship, work to spread the Gospel. [4:5]

Father Algy Robertson, whom I mentioned earlier, was a man of many parts. From the background of a strict evangelical upbringing as a boy, he preached with the enthusiasm of a Billy Graham, and yet managed to combine this with the sacramentalism of an ardent Anglo Catholic. He always, he said, "preached for conversions", and the cutting edge of his ministry, like a two-edged sword, was his profound love for people on the one hand, and his equally profound belief in the Second Coming of our Lord on the other. It was this which gave urgency to his message. Is there not something in this for us? "Little children, it is a last time." There are many situations in our world where that sense of urgency is very real. The sands are running out, the final opportunities being missed. To affirm the immanence of God, in Love and Justice, in the power of His Spirit – "by his coming and his reign" should surely add immediacy to our message. For so many, in many places and under so many conditions of deprivation, violence, and denial of our humanity "the end" is no theological nicety but an immediate reality.

While we, sometimes wearily, drag ourselves through synods, committees, councils, conferences; as the high hopes of our first statements are gradually eroded and modified, rendered pointless and sanitised by drafting and redrafting, amendment on amendment – "here a little and there a little" – so much that was sparkling and fresh echoing the sacred scriptures that are able to make us wise unto salvation which is Christ Jesus, as Paul says here, can seem to be lost. "The time will come," he says, "when they will not stand wholesome teaching, but you yourself must keep calm and sane at all times." [4:3,5]. Keeping calm and sane is not always easy!

Perhaps like him you will have to encourage those who are being engulfed in the turbulent seas of doubt or division to treat you as a rock to which they can turn. To be a source of resolution, faith, patience, love and fortitude, a reliable source of strength.

But because the household of God is being persecuted in

so many places and in so many ways it is necessary also that *we witness* to the Gospel.

When as a boy I travelled every day by tram to school in south London, I passed, at a place called the Elephant and Castle, the very large classical portico with corinthian columns of Spurgeon's Tabernacle. I had no idea who Spurgeon was, or what went on inside the building. Many years later I discovered. When I went to Westcott House I found that the Principal, Ken Carey, had an autograph of the great Spurgeon, framed on the wall of his study, and it reads "the preaching of the everlasting Gospel is the noblest employment of man". I have no doubt this is true. To make known the word and the works of God.

But for it to be true for them, it must first remain the source of our own personal strength to the end of our days. If, like Timothy, you have from early childhood known the sacred writings which are able to make you wise unto salvation which is in Christ Jesus, you will also know that this unfailing source of strength never grows stale, but perpetually renews us in faith and hope and love.

I happened to be sitting next to a rather ageing bishop recently at the Eucharist, and as the New Testament lesson was announced he fished out a tattered and very well worn Greek New Testament and followed a passage, so familiar he must have known it off by heart. It is one way in which we can be assured we will "rise up on wings as eagles" – which I know to be true of him.

Paul is also mindful of the sacrifice which his ministry demands, right to the end. "Already my life is being poured out on the altar," he says [4:6], and the phrase echoes the offering of Jesus. It is true that he would die a martyr's death, and in a sense he is already anticipating that. But the offering of his life had been made from the days of his conversion. I remember very vividly the moment, sitting in a Novice class in Dorset, when I first realised what was commonplace to others – that Jesus on the Cross offered to the Father not only his death but his life. His life blood, everything he had ever been or done from the moment of his birth, all those hidden years, all those brief three years' ministry of preaching, healing, miracle, reconciliation and proclamation of the Kingdom.

Our conversion, too, means nothing less than the continuing offering of ourselves, our souls and bodies to be a reasonable, holy and living sacrifice to God. As the life-blood of Jesus was poured out once for all on the altar of the Cross, so our life is poured out in the arena of this world, and offered daily in union with Him.

If we are to lead our people in penitence then it can only be true if our lives are united with Christ, the Perfect Penitent who for ever pleads for us, and we in him. If we are to lead our people in hope, then it can only be true when we can proclaim as a perpetually renewed wonder "Christ had died, Christ is risen, Christ will come again" in our own lives. If we are to take our people with us to the throne of God, then it will only be true if we have acknowledged in our own lives that "He ever liveth to make intercession for us". Indeed it may be that we will know ourselves to be most truly ourselves when we share with Him in that great work of intercession.

In all Paul's letters there is the mention of so many people, the familiar names of his friends, disciples, the Christian households in which he had stayed; some enemies too! "Alexander the copper-smith did me much harm." It sounds very much like a prayer list – the sort of list I have made more than once, that gets amended, worn out, crossed out, renewed – acting as a goad or a rebuke to my conscience – the people I thought I carried, but who all too frequently have carried me. Lists which force me to face the particularity of God, and as a consequence an inescapable privilege of the priesthood I share with him in Christ Jesus.

To be changed from glory into glory in the spiritual life is also to be renewed from within. The perpetually renewed wonder of approaching the throne of God bringing with us the hopes and loves, the sorrows and needs of the people of God in whose lives we share.

In the interest and pursuit of justice and peace in the world the people of God are increasingly the victims of conflict, their life blood literally poured out. The candle that burns here for Terry Waite and the hostages has its counterpart in Canterbury where the Pope lit a candle in the chapel which commemorates the martyrs of our century. It was not long ago, but the list has grown longer since that day.

For many, many others, whose names are not known by us, the painful reality of Christian witness, of martyrdom, is the witness of daily living. Prayer unites us both with them but also, pre-eminently in the Eucharist, with the victorious offering of the Son of Man.

So much of the hard discussion of the weeks to come will centre on the realities of doctrinal difference, of our refusal to compromise with the material demands of the secular world, on success, or failure in coming to terms with the division in the Church, with other faiths, with the realities of the Third World and so on and so on. Sometimes we will seem to bury our differences certainly in our church services. Yet as the world watches and listens it will instinctively look for something more. This letter to Timothy speaks of "the man who belongs to God" [3:17]. Does that identify the thing, the person for whom they look – even if they don't know it?

There is no blueprint for that. At the heart of prayer is the contemplation of God, consciously, or perhaps at particular times, unconsciously, in our whole lives. Part of the mystery of being is that we already share the eternal heavenly life of the Father and to pray "that we may ever more dwell in him and he in us" is the reality of our life in Christ. Paul says, "The Lord lent me strength so that I might be his instrument in making the full proclamation of the Gospel for the whole pagan world to hear" [4:17]. Surely that is what we want the Anglican Communion to be – His instrument in making the full proclamation of the Gospel.

The ultimate proclamation is in the life of the Church poured out.

According to St John's Gospel, Jesus on the night before his death prayed to his Father, "I have glorified thee on earth having completed the work which thou gavest me to do, and now Father glorify thou me in thy own presence with the glory I had with thee before the world began" [John 17:4].

We are called to glorify God the Father in the particular work he has given us to do. If we are to get it right then the guidelines for glory are contained in the rest of that seventeenth chapter of St John, the great intercessory prayer. It is this that can keep us close to the throne of his glory. The great work is carried forward in the power of prayer.

After some recent examples, the world may be looking for evidence of perestroika, and perhaps at the end of the day we shall chart some changes, make radical moves and so on. What the world will find unanswerable, for it has never properly learnt the language, is clear evidence of the power of prayer in a Church led by men who belong to God, proclaiming with all the people, in spite of everything, "Our God reigns."